Praise for Dear Mr. Wells

As a teacher, principal, and chief school administrator, I firmly believe that multiple copies of this short book should be in every faculty room and professional library in the country. *Dear Mr. Wells* will serve the experienced faculty member and the administrator as an essential tool to impart to the new teacher the real lesson of good teaching, namely to know the student as a person as well as a learner.

—JIM DIRENZO, chief school administrator, Byram Township Schools, Byram Township, New Jersey

I had no intention of reading it in one sitting, but I could not put down this engaging and powerful book. Not only did I appreciate reading the letters from students that Tom included to substantiate the major points he emphasized throughout his book, I also enjoyed his powerful message. His delivery was clear, succinct, and inspirational.

—HELENE COFFIN, teacher and author of *Every Child a Reader*

Tom Wells may be the greatest man, teacher, coach, and mentor I ever had at a very crucial time of my life! I remember vividly many of the life lessons I learned from him.

—JASON PARE, student

I can only hope that every teacher or anyone who wants to be a teacher will read this book. And you do not have to be an educator to both enjoy and appreciate it. But I can tell you, if every teacher focuses on each of their students the way Tom did, those students are going to be very blessed.

—GEORGE SMITH, journalist and book reviewer

I've enjoyed reading *Dear Mr. Wells.* [Tom's] comments are direct, pointed, and specific, supported strongly by the many letters [he references].

—BILL SAYRES, PhD and professor of English

So again, thank you so much from the bottom of my heart for every sleepless night you endured, for every second of your precious time that you willingly gave to all of us, for every single time you didn't let us give up or not give it our all. I know I try to do the same in my classroom—not to say I get it right everyday, but my heart is all in...thanks to teachers like you who lead me by example.

—JENNIFER RASMUSSEN, teacher in Canton, Georgia

I just spent two very emotional hours reading *Dear Mr. Wells.* I proudly admit that I had to reach for the tissues on my desk several times. It will take a little time for me to put in words the many thoughts that are running through my head.

The majority of books about teaching and learning miss the most important factors that determine success. A successful teacher must be passionate about students and making a difference. Tom does an excellent job of highlighting those concepts succinctly and accurately.

Tom made me realize how much I miss being with kids every day. This book should be required reading for all teachers and anyone considering entering the profession. If the reader is not moved by Tom's story and the mutual love and respect between Tom and his students, they may want to reconsider their career choice.

Any educator who reads this book will experience the same emotional roller coaster I did and will be rejuvenated and empowered to continue in the most important and noblest profession—teaching!

Additionally, I think anyone who cares about our educational system (which includes parents, taxpayers, politicians, and students) would benefit from reading this book and understanding its message.

—JIM ANASTASIO, superintendent, Augusta Schools

Dear Mr. Wells

His students speak

Tom Wells

Designed and produced by:
Maine Authors Publishing
12 High Street, Thomaston, Maine
www.maineauthorspublishing.com

Printed in the United States of America

Dedication

I dedicate this book to all educators who spend countless hours connecting with kids and mentoring them. Not only do they teach their subject matter, but more importantly they help provide kids with the tools to become happy, respectful, productive adults. Despite the distractions, you play a critical role, and I am proud to call you my peers.

Proceeds from the sale of this book will go toward a scholarship in the name of Barbara Haskell, an integral member of our Cony High School faculty, who recently lost her battle with leukemia.

Table of Contents

Preface

Why Teach?
Just Ask a Student

Dear Mr. Wells,

This is your window into our perspective—this retirement gift's purpose is to let you see yourself with our eyes. It's our humble attempt to give you the kind of recognition you have so generously given us, time and time again—to bear witness to your accomplishments, the wisdom you shared, and the gestures of kindness you showed us. It's not only a collection of letters; it's a collection of our gratitude.

This portfolio was created to say thank you...not just for teaching us how to write, or run, or any of the other numerous things we learned from you, but for being you. Thanks for calling kids "dumbass," joking around, and smiling constantly. Thanks for not having any tolerance for bullshit, respecting us, and treating us like young adults, not kids. Thanks for showing interest in your students and genuinely caring about our well-being, for having an open-door policy and making time to just chat with us. Thank you for lifting our spirits, building our confidence, and believing in us.

We want to thank you for enriching our lives.

I don't believe there is one world, just seven billion interpretations of it; change one person's interpretation and you have changed the world, one mind at a time. That's how you are engraved in our memory—changing our world through your guidance, support, and kindness.

I hope, as you learn how we remember our time together, you are also able to think back on your own memories.

My wish is that when you open this book, you are reminded of all the writing conferences, all the letters of recommendation, all the practices, cross country meets, track meets, wrestling meets, football games, whitewater raft trips, Chizzle Wizzle performances, and *Rameses* issues. I hope it reminds you of the lessons you taught, as well as the ones you learned. I hope it reminds you of your classrooms and the kids that filled them each and every day. I hope it helps you remember how much you made us smile, and all the hugs you gave—because, in the end, they hold more value than grades.

But above all, I hope every time you open this book, you will feel the love and gratitude we will always have for you. Our teacher. Our mentor. Our friend."

Gratefully yours,
Heather

Incredulously, I stared at the thick, three-ring binder sitting in front of me containing eighty-eight pages of thank-you's and congratulatory notes from past students, every one of them proving one thing to me: Teachers make a difference and kids actually appreciate our hard work and mentorship.

This is why *we* teach; we do make a difference. Sometimes, it's life-changing…and many times we don't even realize it. It is imperative that teachers know that they are the key to our future.

We make indelible impressions on our students and hold the key (along with their families) to their success and happiness. It has always held true, now more than ever. It is my goal that this book helps put things into perspective for all teachers, for all parents, for all students— for everyone. More importantly, I hope that I can help highlight for all the integral role good teachers play in helping kids transition into satisfied, meaningful adults, ones who make good choices and respect both themselves and others.

My students' insights also define the qualities that characterize effective educators. From their lips we (teachers, teachers-to-be) learn. What does it take to reach *all* students? How does a competent teacher help students with the challenges of growing up?

Read on….

CHAPTER I

Retirement Must Wait

I...*must*...write...this...book.

I recently retired after forty-one years of teaching, each and every minute spent in the same school system. There are many explanations why I stayed put (perhaps no one else would have me), but my topic is not *my* school; it's all schools. My topic is not me; it's all good educators. Most importantly, though, my topic is education and the role it plays in the successful development of our students: It has the power to change the world.

The fact is, like all good teachers, I love kids—their innocence, their bravado, their naivete, their energy—and I also love teaching. It's an art. Never did it cross my mind to enter another vocation (even though my starting yearly salary was $8500...a year).

Evidence of my love of teaching is my retirement letter. It was one of the toughest "writing assignments" I have ever had, but it is a true reflection of how I feel about the teaching profession.

January 1, 2014
James Anastasio, Superintendent of Schools
Augusta School District
12 Gedney Street
Augusta, ME 04330

Dear Jim,

It is with fond memories and a heavy heart that I am announcing my retirement from the Augusta school district effective the end of this school year. After forty-one years of service, I feel that it is time to begin the next phase of my life.

I have thoroughly enjoyed working for the system. Suffice it to say that Cony High School is my second home and that my tenure here has been rewarding. Working with a professional staff that truly cares about kids has been an experience I would not trade for anything.

From my first year fresh out of Bates College forty-one years ago, I have worked alongside passionate educators, I have taught students who care about learning and care about each other, I have worked with administrators who trust and support their faculty, and I have partnered with parents who have made their child's education a priority. This is the combination that makes a school successful—and special.

Each day I have hopped in my car, looking forward to seeing my students and fellow teachers. The entire school system has been creative and supportive, making sure that every student has an advocate—that students have a teacher who cares about them and is willing to do anything to see them succeed. This is showcased in the smile of every teenager who walks the halls of Cony.

I write this letter on New Year's Day, knowing that it is time for me to begin a new phase of my life. My decision is bittersweet: I am leaving a job I love and students who mean more to me than most anything (with the exception of my family), but I will be entering an era with new opportunities and challenges. I am excited, but I will miss my students. I will miss my colleagues. I will miss my classroom. I will miss the Cony experience.

I hope that I have played a part in helping the Augusta School System become the hard-working, positive, and caring institution that it is. Thank you for the opportunity.

Sincerely,
Thomas D. Wells

It's kids that have brought me joy, brought me fulfillment, and brought meaning to my life, and there is little doubt now the relationship is reciprocal. Until recently, I did not realize the impact teachers have on their students. I always sensed it but was too busy working on my lesson plans and common assessments or reading myriad essays to put much thought into it until now.

Just prior to my retirement I was given a precious gift that motivated me to write this book. A former student, Heather Leet, along with a friend in my English department, Laurie Rodrigue, decided to lead the charge in the creation of my retirement gift. Together, they compiled congratulatory notes from previous students and created my "writing portfolio," a three-ring binder filled with insights that validated my teaching career. Contributors were instructed to handwrite or type out their well wishes and send them to Heather and Laurie.

My retirement gift, my cherished "writing portfolio," opened my eyes. It became my favorite "textbook," teaching *me* the most important lesson of my career—good teachers are game changers. The brown three-ring binder displayed a gold plate mounted on the cover. The inscription read: "Life sucks and then you retire, dumbass. Tom's writing portfolio." It was eighty-eight pages long, filled with meaningful insights from students dating back to the early 1980s. While reading it, I decided that I must give it a fitting name. Because of its powerful message captured by students, I now call it, "The Educational Bible According to Students."

I know the original title sounds crude and unprofessional, but ironically it defines my life as a teacher and represents one of my teaching "techniques" that has proven successful. In the portfolio itself, I have dozens of students who thank me for my "gruffness" and my approach that includes telling kids to "suck it up" and get to work. Teaching is all about forming strong relationships, and I learned far more in my own classroom than I did in college. It's called on-the-job training.

On my teaching journey, I discovered that if I could forge positive relationships with my students, then they would learn. Interestingly, they not only absorb necessary knowledge about my subject (English), but also they learn about life. They experience success and happiness. I was not only a teacher, but an important mentor as well.

While reading their insights, I realized that being a positive role model for them was far more important than teaching them how to write clearly and concisely. They appreciated my challenging class, my love and respect for them, and my unending journey to try and connect with each one.

One recent experience captures what I mean, and why my portfolio carries its rather crude nameplate. It also illustrates the qualities that help in the development of these relationships that allow teachers to impact their students.

Dumbass

Kim, my principal, called me into her office one day and asked me if I would be interested in teaching Freshman English, a newly formed class that included ninth graders who struggled (and some who failed) eighth grade Language Arts. The group included kids with behavior problems, kids who hated school, and kids who struggled academically as well. It was an attempt to bring these students together and help them experience success, something that was foreign to them. The rest of the freshmen class would be taking English I.

Kim's question was more of a directive, but she knew that I would say yes, because I love teaching, no matter who is occupying the seats before me. She was relieved, said thanks, and I was on my merry way.

Well, the class, though small (fourteen students) was "interesting." It consisted of intelligent kids with attitudes, kids from broken homes, kids who were cocky because they played a sport, and kids with little to no self-esteem. It was a tad different from my AP English class the following period, but I like all teens and looked forward to the challenge.

I treated this class like all the rest, forging positive relationships with each and every one of them. I made it my mission to get to know their likes/dislikes, their choice of friends, and their hobbies—connecting with them on a personal level. I gathered this information using a number of methods, the most accurate technique: *eavesdropping.* I would follow them closely down the hall and listen to their conversations, which allowed me to understand them and ask rather interesting questions when they entered my class.

I also had them write their biographies (thank goodness I am an English teacher), and from all this information, I was able to begin to forge positive relationships. I would become one of them, so we could connect, and that each one knew that I liked them.

They knew that I cared.

About three months passed and we were working on a writing assignment, an expository piece that answered a question about a novel we were reading. They seemed to be working diligently while I sauntered up and down the rows answering questions. Out of nowhere, Billy, a young man who played basketball, broke the silence by screaming (yes, screaming), "This is so stupid. Why are we doing this? It's dumb."

The rest of the students looked to me for a reaction. They were scared, thinking I would send him to the office for disciplining. I must admit, he was a challenge the previous month, but I had been doing my best to connect with him. Knowing that he loved basketball, I read the newspaper every day and kept track of his games and the points he scored. Constantly, I would ask him about his recent experiences on the team, and every day we talked basketball before he walked into my room.

At the time of his outburst, however, I wasn't thinking basketball. I looked at Billy, and calmly asked, "What's the problem? Why do you think it's stupid?"

He replied, "This has nothing to do with me. It's just stupid. I hate it!"

After taking a deep breath, I attempted to explain about the role of writing in life, how communication is one of the major keys to success. I gave him my best lines, so to speak, even citing specific examples of how writing strengthens communication skills and is marketable. I even advised Billy that communication skills would help him get a date. (Yes, I was getting desperate!)

He continued to give me a hard time, however. Losing my patience, I quickly and authoritatively said, "Billy, stop behaving like a dumbass*." I heard a gasp travel throughout the classroom.

He glared at me from his desk, and shouted, "Did you hear that? Wells just called me an ass. What's up with that?"

Before I could do or say anything, almost as if on cue, a cute girl in the row next to him blurted out, "It's because you are behaving like one."

He turned to her with a horrified look on his face. The class was silent. Tension filled the air. Billy, so surprised that a fellow classmate (yet alone a cute girl) put him in his place, did not say a word. Before the rest of the students could say anything, I announced, "OK, class, continue with your essays until the bell rings. Individually, I will call each of you to my desk and we will have writing conferences. Now get back to work."

So, weeks flew by, and I continued to try to form a positive relationship with Billy, never mentioning the "ass incident." I said hi in the hallways when we passed and kept track of his basketball career. In class, he performed well, and it was obvious that he was trying. About two months passed, and he was working so hard that I approached his coach and told him that Billy was the most improved student in my class. I asked the coach to take him aside and praise him on his accomplishment, which he did on the bus on the way to a basketball game. Reporting back to me, coach shared that Billy had a huge smile on his face after the "announcement."

We continued to work at our relationship for the remainder of the year. Before summer break, we said our goodbyes, pretty much putting the "dumbass" episode in the history books.

A year later, Billy entered my room, looked me in the face, and said, "Mr. Wells, would you be able to come to the game on Tuesday night? Each basketball player is choosing his favorite teacher to be recognized at half-time, and I chose you. Is that OK?"

Trying to hide my excitement, I said, "I'd be honored, Billy. Thank you." But inside I was overwhelmed with a feeling I just can't describe, and it's those feelings/connections that make teaching the best of professions. Once we establish these relationships, the sky's the limit. Billy is now a junior and is already making plans for college. In contrast, he started his freshman year a young, angry man who hated school and whose only concern was what was for lunch. Go figure.

This incident is representative of how I teach and how I form relationships with students. It's real; it's rough; it's tough love. And more importantly it's one piece of proof that teachers make a difference. It works, and it is the reason why my retirement gift/portfolio has its crude inscription. The English department presented me with this priceless gift just days before the end of the school year, and the end of my career, and in it I found the greatest lesson of all.

*Dumbass is a term often used by a character from one of my favorite TV shows, *That '70s Show*. In it, a father called Red Foreman felt it necessary to be a strict, cantankerous parent/friend. He used to call his kids and friends "dumbass" when lecturing them, but it was apparent that—in a weird way—it was a term of endearment, a way to show that he cared for them.

CHAPTER 2

Teaching 101

It's students like Billy who contributed to my retirement gift, which without a doubt, validated my teaching career. The letters eloquently captured how I had affected students' lives. The portfolio flashed back dozens of years, some entries written by adults who are now in their fifties (many are parents of my current students). What truly moved me was the fact that no one was *forced* to write their thoughts—they *wanted* to. As adults (through their eyes as teens), they realized I made a difference in their lives. Their writing was bittersweet, oftentimes laced with humor. As portfolio contributor Sam Hopkins put it, "Gratitude and appreciation are such simple things, but *damn*, they're hard to put into words..."

I realize that there may be naysayers out there who might state, "Hell, you had thousands of students. Not many replied..."

Interesting point, but think about this. Very few actually received the message, and out of those, many have lives that don't permit them to sit down and reflect, yet alone write. Out of respect for them, they have commitments—jobs, kids, families—and they were asked to handwrite/type their notes. Let's be real, folks. I'm not sure I could have accepted this assignment either.

Not only have I received written messages, but I have also been personally contacted by students thanking me for giving them the tools to survive (no hyperbole here). Some have beaten cancer; some have just beaten the odds, so to speak. I will share their stories later....

So, after receiving my precious retirement gift, I returned to my classroom, anxious to dive into its contents. With care (after laughing at the inscription on the nameplate), I opened it and began to read the first letter. Immediately I felt my throat begin to tighten and my eyes tear up. I became short of breath. I then realized that sitting before me was something more special than anything I could have imagined.

The very first "letter" was from a student I had in my last class just prior to retirement. Jonas was a guitar player with long red hair, not terribly motivated in school. His note began, "You probably get hundreds of these every year. You probably hear this a million times from a million students. And truthfully, mine probably won't stand out to you. But I want to write it anyway.

"I want to thank you for keeping me going."

The rest of his thank-you focused on how I changed his life. I thought to myself, "Did this truly happen? Jonas is a great kid, someone I really liked and connected with. I didn't realize that he was struggling to this degree."

So I continued reading and was overwhelmed by the power of his message. Feeling wrought with emotion, I closed my bible and choked back the tears. Short of breath, I leaned back in my chair to compose myself. A wave of nostalgia flooded my senses, and all of a sudden I was overcome with happiness and fulfillment.

I reopened my bible and continued reading his message.

It took me an hour to finish the first submission. During that time, I not only reflected on the message, but also was moved beyond words. It seemed that after each paragraph, I reacted the same way. I would close my eyes and fondly remember the writer. I would then create an image of him/her sitting in my classroom, right down to the clothes they used to wear. At that point, I would begin to capture the emotional connection we had. And without exception, my last reaction was much the same, and wonderfully fulfilling.

I would get short of breath, my throat would tighten, and tears would run freely. To a T, each letter overwhelmed me with its message.

The second letter was written by an AP student, who was also the class valedictorian and daughter of my principal. It began with, "I hated you at first. I hated the way you wouldn't give me an A. I hated the way you expected way more from me than any other teacher. I hated the way you made me really have to think and focus on understanding things. I hated your dumb jokes and your occasional crudeness. Now that the year is coming to a close, however, those are all the reasons I will miss you most. I don't hate you anymore. In fact, I think you are the greatest teacher I have ever had."

Filled with happiness (and nostalgia), I finally began to reflect on my many years teaching. The portfolio sitting in front of me was validation for a career that I truly loved, a career that gave me far more than I could possible put into words, a career that was more meaningful than life itself.

I then had an epiphany (which is somewhat atypical for me): This portfolio could belong to *any* good teacher. It was filled with notes to *all* teachers, not just me. These "kids" are *their* students who finally have an opportunity to thank them. Their insights might be from an older perspective now, but they captured the influence good teachers have. These notes highlight students' feelings, their insights, and their appreciation for what teachers do. These "kids" wrote with such power, such fervor, and also supplied concrete evidence that we have helped change the world. It took me nine months to read every contribution, not because there are thousands, but because every single one of them was so moving.

And meaningful.

They proved to me that an effective educator is worth her weight in gold. According to Nicole Liyange-Don, a 2012 graduate of my high school, "With rueful disappointment, I constantly lament the regrettable lack of recognition good teachers receive. It's a shame that, unlike nations like Finland and South Korea, the United States does not afford teachers the same prestige and respect granted to doctors and lawyers. You undoubtedly deserve it."

So I am going to use their own words to capture the life-changing influence teachers have. Their insights will prove that we do make a difference, even though we sometimes have the government, school boards, and parents all telling us that we don't. There are countless books that prove, through empirical data and research, that a good education is important and helps provide tools for success. I am not going to quote them. I am not going to use data. I am going to use something more convincing than hard numbers.

My "data" is kids. After all, aren't they the ones to which the research applies? I believe they will not only validate the evidence, but "put a face" on the reality that good teachers play a monumental role in a kid's life.

Students appreciate what we do for them, even though they don't realize it immediately, because their lives get in the way. Do you remember those years? As teenagers, they don't have the time or energy to tell us. At this point in their lives, they don't realize the impact teachers have. Bret LaForge, class of 2011 says it best: "I've come to realize just how many things in my life you've had a hand in since I graduated—without even knowing it."

So it's a catch-22. We don't have time to reflect on our meaningful careers, and kids don't have time to show their appreciation. Rebecca Sproul, class of 2014, nails it: "All the work, effort, and time [teachers] put into making us great is appreciated, even though we rush out the door without actually saying so."

I find it most powerful that my "students" were not forced to write these notes. They are not sitting in front of me in a crowded classroom. It is not a homework assignment. They are now adults, busy with college, with jobs, with families, with the demands of life. Finding the time to capture their insights must have been challenging, but they felt it necessary that I know that I impacted their lives and—in a couple of cases—saved them.

To me, this collection proves that good teachers connect with kids and help them figure out the mysteries of life. The problem is that we just can't see beyond the next standardized test or performance indicator. We must not lose sight of why we teach—to help kids. We can't forget that the most important choice we can make as teachers is to respect kids and form positive relationships with each and every one of them.

We must stop looking over our shoulders and realize that we must focus on what is most important, sitting directly in front of us: our students.

One contributor to my portfolio in particular, Veronica Swain, highlighted what's happening in today's classroom because of the pressures placed on teachers, ones that diminish their performance. "Teachers in public schools have plenty of pressure on them in terms of conforming to the system and avoiding administrative pressures. I suppose this is why so many well-meaning public servants turn into the lifeless rule-followers that students everywhere have come to know and loathe."

Ouch.

However, my retirement portfolio is evidence that we do make a difference, but we can't be afraid. We can't let the system distract us from our mission. We must stay true to who we are and teach kids, not just teach material. We play a major part in the drama of life: an integral mentor who helps our students face their trials and tribulations and evolve into successful and happy human beings.

What is more important than that?

This book is my gift to a career that transcends the trivialities of politics, of educational movements, of people who don't know the true challenges we face. Teachers must believe in their class, their message, and their meaningful role in a student's life. As student Jennifer Moody, class of 2000, puts it, "As we move through life and its many stages, certain roots that were planted along the way help us to stay strong and brave the storm. Teachers are one of the greatest contributors to those roots, the lessons taught to us with attention, care, and dedication."

With the publication of this book, it is my goal to have "no teacher left behind."

CHAPTER 3

Dumbass Luck

I have always loved teaching, but it was never my intent to become an educator. So why did I enter this noblest of professions? How did I end up a teacher for forty-one years in a profession that has given me more than I could ever have asked for? There is a simple answer: dumbass luck.

From the very beginning of my life, without knowing it, I was developing the most important quality that would help me become a successful teacher: the ability to understand and connect with my students.

I was born in Brooklyn, New York, one of seven children. I had two older sisters, three younger brothers, and one younger sister. We moved out of New York City when I was two, to a small town (population about 5,000) called Montrose, about forty miles north, which overlooked the Hudson River. My dad commuted by train to the city each day, while my mom was left home to manage a rather large family. It was "interesting" being a member, but I firmly believe this was the beginning of my teaching training: learning how to get along with others.

I was a "normal" male at that time, one who wanted to do as little work as possible, one who liked sports and extracurricular activities, one who loved his social life more than reading *Romeo and Juliet*. Like today's teens, I also wanted to be attractive to the opposite sex and once in a while had a steady girlfriend. Everything I experienced in both high school and college has allowed me to relate to my own students.

After graduating from Hendrick Hudson High School, a cocky I-can-do-anything teenage boy who felt invincible, I attended Bates College in Lewiston, Maine. I went to college because that's what people did after attending high school. Ironically, I chose Bates, a prestigious liberal arts college, out of laziness.

Not wanting to put any work into the college application process (after all, sports and hanging with my friends were far more important) I applied to the same colleges my older sister did. I visited the campuses (because my parents strongly suggested it) and filled out my applications. I received acceptance letters from two (Bates and Dickinson College in Pennsylvania), and I was wait-listed at Dartmouth.

I chose Bates because it had a better track team, and I was passionately in love with pole vaulting. Like most teenage males, we love something because it is good to us and loves us back. For whatever reason, I was a talented pole-vaulter in high school, and to this day I firmly believe it is the reason why I was accepted into a competitive college. I did earn decent grades in high school, but not good enough to get into "big name" colleges, at least not without a little help.

Pole-vaulting provided that help.

So in 1972 off to college I went. My mom and dad deposited me in front of my dorm in Maine and away they went, back to New York to my six brothers and sisters. Standing on campus taking in the sights, I never once thought that in four short years I would be standing in *front* of a classroom. The journey was an interesting one, atypical to say the least.

Like many other freshmen, my first year was a struggle…academically. High school was easy for me, and I had not developed the time management skills I needed in a competitive college setting. Following first semester, I was placed on academic probation, a real eye-opener. I buckled down and performed better in the classroom, still paying ample attention to sports and my social life (and girls in particular, with whom I had little success).

I continued on my path the next couple of years, performing satisfactorily in the classroom and finding success in football and indoor and outdoor track. By the end of my sophomore year I had declared my major: psychology. It comes as no surprise, I'm sure, that my reason was consistent with most of the rationale behind my previous decisions: I had heard that it was the easiest major at Bates. I had no "plans" for this major, just that I found it interesting and fairly nonthreatening. Teaching had not yet entered the picture by the end of my sophomore year. During that time, I also loaded up with English classes because I always loved to read, even though writing was not my strong suit. I fell in love with this many years later.

My junior year proceeded in much the same manner, but by January, I realized (with the help of my parents) that I did not want to choose psychology as a career, mainly because it would require more schooling (yuck). I then had an important decision to make: my lifelong occupation. Having a fondness for reading, I decided to declare my minor, English. This is not particularly marketable, so I added a focus on education. At a small liberal arts college like Bates, they did not offer an education *major*, but they provided enough classes in education so that students could earn certification in their major/minor.

So, initially, I did not have a true passion to become a teacher. It turned out that I did not choose education; it chose me.

Dumbass luck strikes again.

And at this point in time in my life I wouldn't change a thing. Ironically, I must get the word out that this profession is truly meaningful, and I owe it to the educational world—and more importantly to kids—to convince worthy individuals to become a part of our faculty, so to speak.

My junior year in college was my turning point, and off I went into the study of education, without a clue about where it would take me. Without thinking (Remember, I'm a male growing up in a time when we didn't have to think or feel.) I chose a career that would ultimately bring me profound happiness and fulfillment.

Go figure. Lady Luck continued to wave her magic wand.

Even after my first few education classes, I did not develop an urge to become a teacher. They made sense, and unlike in today's college classroom, I did not face the myriad requirements: memorize hundreds of terms, educational standards, learning standards, and other assorted protocols. I loved student-teaching at Lewiston Junior High School, which was just down the street from the Bates campus. I had a great mentor who gave me unheard of freedom in her classroom and, more importantly, wrote a wonderful recommendation when I began to apply for a job.

My silly luck does not end there. It played a huge role in getting my first (and only) teaching job. I believe that God also played a role in this.

The middle of my senior year at Bates, I sent out ninety applications and received three interviews. (Teaching was a very competitive field in 1976.) I travelled far and wide (Farmington, Connecticut; Londonderry, New Hampshire; and Bath, Maine) hoping that one of these school systems would hire me. No such luck this time.

But wait….

In May, while taking my last class at Bates, I got a call from my football coach. He was directing a clinic for Maine high school coaches, and he asked me if I would help him.

My role was minimal; I was to be his guinea pig and act out many of the moves he was describing to the group of high school football coaches. Because I was tight with my coach, I agreed (reluctantly, since it would make me miss an important party). Ironically, the clinic was being held at Bowdoin College, our archrival.

We arrived and set up; I was a bit apprehensive that my coach would notice that I was a tad hungover. Nonetheless, the clinic proceeded without a hitch, and immediately prior to the end of the event, he announced, "By the way, this young man (pointing at me) is looking for a teaching job. If you have any leads that might help him, it would be much appreciated."

A short, burly man then approached me and said, "Hi. My name is John Dudley, and I was just hired as the head football coach at Cony High School."

I had no idea where the heck that was, but I didn't care.

He continued, "I am looking for an assistant coach. Cony has had a woeful program, and I have been hired to turn it around. I just won two state championships at Morse High School [ironically, one of the three schools to which I applied] and Cony believes I am their man. Oh, by the way, I think the junior high school is looking for an English teacher."

"Funny," I thought, "He just implied that teaching is the extracurricular activity." (I soon found he indeed felt this way.)

Consequently, it turned out that after sending out ninety applications, receiving three interviews, and not being offered a job, some school in Augusta, Maine, needed a football coach, and also an English teacher.

Lady Luck calls again!

With few expectations, I applied and got an interview, which represented another huge stroke of luck. Walking nervously into my interview, I noticed five older adults sitting around a large table. They welcomed me, and the person at the head pointed to my seat. Walking nervously to the end of the table, I felt a tad intimidated, but tried to put on my confident mask. The butterflies in my stomach were having a feeding frenzy, but ignoring them, I sat down, straightened up tall, and puffed out my chest.

The committee began to describe the job.

After reviewing the typical aspects of a junior high English teacher, they shared some interesting information with me. It turned out that they desperately wanted to start a wrestling program, and I had wrestled in high school. Looking at my résumé, one interviewer asked about whether I would be willing to start a wrestling program at the high school. Even though I hadn't seen a mat in four years, with an air of confidence and conviction, I replied, "Absolutely, it's a wonderful sport."

The hiring committee all nodded their heads at once. Some even tried to hide the slight smiles that appeared on their faces. I was feeling a little more confident.

After perusing my application, another interviewer on the committee asked about my writing experience, particularly regarding publication. I weakly replied, "I wrote an article for the school paper."

"Well, great," he replied with glee, "We need a school newspaper advisor as well. Would you be willing to fill that position?"

I was beginning to think that it was my destiny to teach for the Augusta School System, even though I needed a map to find it just thirty miles away from Bates.

Lastly, I came to find out that Lady Luck had been also watching me during my student teaching at Lewiston Junior High School. Apparently, the principal at the junior high school to which I was now applying had held an administrative position in Lewiston years earlier. He knew my host teacher, who wrote a glowing recommendation, and I truly believe this is what convinced the hiring committee to offer me the job.

Lady Luck at her best.

My search for my one and only job turned out to be the perfect storm, nothing of which had to do with a passion for teaching.

Thus, my career began, and—in reflecting—I couldn't have been happier (or luckier).

It was then time to begin to learn how to become an effective educator. My on-the-job training was about to begin. My own students would become my second family, and together we would learn. I would teach them how to read analytically and write effectively, and they would teach me that a caring educator helps provide the keys to success and happiness.

CHAPTER 4

It's More Than the Portfolio

For the most part, I will be relying on my "Dumbass Portfolio" to prove that teachers make a difference, but things keep happening in my life that help me understand the pivotal role we play in the lives of our "kiddos." I will also include anecdotes that will serve as proof as well. Years after their graduation, I often run into them, and they have profound stories to share involving my role in their lives. It happens more and more....

A recent event motivated me beyond a shadow of a doubt to write a book for teachers, showing them that despite all the "protocol" that gets in the way (No Child Left Behind, Learning Targets, PLP's, SAT's, IEP's, etc.) they must not forget that their job is to spin positive relationships. They must remember that they are in the classroom for one reason, and one reason only—their students. They must become their mentors.

A couple of weeks ago, I received a message from a student of mine (Dana) who graduated 25 years ago. She told me that her brother Mike, whom I taught and coached, was diagnosed with cancer. Dana wanted me to know that at a gathering of close friends many stories were shared and a fair amount of them included Mike's athletic career, and my name came up often. She informed me that Mike might enjoy a quick note from me.

I jumped at the chance. So, I sent him a quick email, kind of testing the waters:

> Mike, just heard about your battle, and I had to write to see how you are doing. Saw your picture on the Gofundme page, and I'd have to say that you look great with a bald head!

Seeing your image brought back countless memories, all good. It appears that you still are focused, strong, and doing great things because of these traits. You haven't changed a bit, and it doesn't surprise me that you have achieved such success and are taking your battle with cancer head on.

Please keep me posted on your progress, because you mean a lot to me. I want you to know that I love you and believe in you.

Your old fart coach,
Tom Wells (yes, you can call me Tom!)"

I received a quick reply, and his message proves that we teachers/coaches have a monumental impact on our students.

Hi, Tom!

Very happy to receive your email and really appreciate you taking the time to reach out.

Yes, it's been a bit of a roller coaster with my diagnosis. I'll keep it short and look to bring you up to date. In late October I was feeling great, training on a regular basis, doing judo, and preparing for a charity bike ride that runs the length of Cape Cod. Closing our training facility one night, I went to the rest room and noted my urine was straight blood. Bit of a shocker. However, having no other symptoms (pain, lethargy, unexplained weight loss, etc.), I did the race and also contacted my doc.

After a few tests, it was determined I had a large tumor in my right kidney (7.5cm). The good news at the time was the tumor was encapsulated, or limited to only the kidney. Normal procedure is to remove the kidney, and the majority of the time the patient moves on with no further issues. Subsequently, I had the tumor removed mid-November. We believed the issue to be resolved and told my staff, as I would be out for a week or so. Things seemed to go smoothly when we hosted Thanksgiving and travelled to Dana's home in Texas for Christmas.

Early January I was feeling as if my progress was slowing and I was actually feeling worse. Tests showed in the eight weeks since the initial CT scan that the cancer (renal cell carcinoma) had metastasized to my stomach, liver, and right lung. I was immediately referred to a local oncologist who then referred me to Dana-Farber Cancer Institute in Boston. There were some fights with the insurance company, etc., but I'm happy to say I'm receiving great care.

I've had two treatments of immunotherapy (once every three weeks) in a clinical trial, and the results so far have been exceptional. I'm feeling better, with an increase in energy and appetite. While I'm down 45 pounds from my normal 195, I feel I am getting better every day. I could wrestle at this weight; however, most twelve- or thirteen-year-olds could probably kick my butt—LOL.

The support my family and I have received from our family, friends, local community, and past communities such as Tufts has been overwhelming at times. Learning how to accept the generosity in all its forms has been one of the biggest lessons of my life. I probably don't need to tell you the reward I feel when I receive an email from an athlete I worked with twenty-five years ago about how much I made a positive impact on him, and the bigger kick comes when he is now passing that same lesson on to his children. *We, as coaches and teachers, can never underestimate the value of a simple act.*

I feel very strongly any success I have today as a coach, a teacher, a friend, a husband, and a father was influenced in some way through my relationship with you, Tom. I truly enjoyed everything in my life, including the bumps in the road such as this one. You taught me to consistently give the best of myself on every effort, and I believe that has made all the difference.

With honor and love,
Mike

This is not an isolated incident, either. Granted, if I can affect just one person to this magnitude, my teaching career was worth it, but now that I'm retired, this happens every year; it happens every month; it happens every week.

The sad part is I never realized the impact I had on my students, and many of today's teachers have become far too distracted by their extra duties to see the impact they've had sitting right in front of them.

Just two days ago (January 17, 2018) I received a call from one of my students who graduated in 2010. Chris and I were quite close, because he loved producing rap music and its lyrics, and this was similar to poetry, which I taught in his class. Excitedly, he informed me that he had scored a job hauling lobster traps off the coast of Maine, and that he also was still rapping. Pretty much out of the blue he informed me that he wrote a song that included me.

I began to reflect back to our relationship. I remembered Chris well because he was struggling and captured it in his music. I created a strong bond, and we became close. He knew I cared and he needed that. Eventually, he graduated and sporadically he returned to talk, but I didn't know that he was struggling with huge issues like addiction.

Directly after our conversation, I excitedly visited his online webpage at christopherscottseesmusic.com. Searching the contents, I came upon his most recent production. I clicked on the song, and immediately was transported back to his high school years. What truly overwhelmed me were the lyrics that were screaming from his page. At first they captured his struggle, and then they highlighted the important role I played in his life and proved that teachers make monumental differences, at times without even knowing it. Reflecting on our relationship, he wrote:

> And back in high school, this teacher thought high of me
> It gassed me up; I liked being thought high of
> Years passed, was in some shit and wasn't being myself
> Stopped in every now and then, even those few minutes helped
> Friends had left me stranded, the home was damaged and I felt
> Abandoned
> But I never discussed this with the man and
> It's been a while since I've stopped in though he's asked
> I was busy looking for treasure, sorting through trash
> But at last I fled that life and moved on
> He was the first I wanted to tell, second to Mom
> But now he's gone, not dead yet, but he's moved
> If I ever see him again, I'll tell him this too.

And he has.

More recently (two weeks ago) Chris contacted me and said he had a two-week vacation and wanted to get together to catch up. He invited me for breakfast at a local diner in Brunswick, about forty miles away. I was anxious to visit with him and hear about his journey the last eight years.

Walking into the diner, it was not hard to pick him out. Standing there with his short dark hair and rather Asian appearance, he hadn't changed a bit. His slight frame approached me and excitedly he said, "What's up, man? Good to see you, Mr. Wells!"

We hugged, and the waitress seated us. Excitedly, I asked, "Do you mind if I record this on my phone? I'm in the process of writing a book about teaching, and I might want to use some of your story."

Chris replied quickly, "A book? That's so cool, man. Sure, you can tape this. Go for it, dude!"

I asked him what he had been up to since the last time I saw him, and he took no time filling me in. He had moved around a lot, wanting to pursue his music career, but with no success. He had gotten involved with a number of things, most of which were not good for him. Through the constant support from his mother, and some true soul searching, he had turned things around and now was working as a sternman on a lobster boat. He genuinely loved the work and his coworkers, and he was feeling great about himself.

At the end of the story, he looked at me and said, "Mr. Wells. Do you know what made the difference? Do you know what helped me turn things around and take responsibility to feel good about my life?"

I wasn't sure I wanted to know, but he was on a roll and needed to talk, so I said, "No, Chris, but I'd love to know what could have done that. Perhaps we can bottle it and sell it for a million dollars." (I often use humor to cover up when I'm in emotional territory and feeling uncomfortable.)

Chris looked me directly in my eyes and said, "You."

I felt my heart rush and began to sweat. Short of breath, I replied, "When did I do that? I haven't seen you in forever."

He didn't hesitate, replying, "When I used to visit you the year after I graduated, I was in a bad place. I wanted to talk with you but didn't want to let you in on my little secret. I told you that I was moving around a lot, from college to college. I continued telling you of my exploits, and you said something that I never forgot and started to live by recently."

I was anxious to find out. "What the heck was that, Chris?"

Leaning forward, he said slowly and with conviction, "When I was telling you about what I was doing, you said to me, 'Chris, it sounds to me like you are running away from something. It sounds like you are looking for a positive change by going to different places. If I were you, I'd stop expecting to have the places change you. Only you have the power to make a difference. Nothing else.'"

Quite honestly, I did not remember giving him this advice, but I didn't have a great deal of time to think, because he followed his previous statement with this: "And every time I felt myself using excuses and blaming everyone else for my shortcomings, I thought of this, and that is the reason I am here today, confident and happy with my life."

Turning off my tape recorder, I stared proudly at Chris. The connection I created with him as a young adult proved to be just what was needed to help him with important issues in his life. Yes, I helped make him a better writer; yes, I helped him with his rap lyrics; yes, I provided a listening ear. But more importantly, I not only provided a mentor whom he could trust and emulate, I (without knowing it) helped him make life-changing decisions when he was mature enough to figure it out.

Yes, Chris had become my teacher, and the lesson was an enjoyable one. Like many of my students, he opened my eyes to the reality of the power of an effective educator. It is my goal to show society (through my students' insights) that we not only help kids learn our subject matter, but we also provide pieces to the puzzle of life.

CHAPTER 5

The Noblest of Professions

I was lucky to retire with enough energy to reflect on my teaching career and realize that I truly made a difference in my students' lives, all 6,000+ of them.

My retirement prompted me to explore the question: "*Why* did I spend my entire life teaching? *What* was the attraction? *Why* do I love kids?" I thought it funny that I hadn't given it much thought. Until recently, I set my professional life on autopilot. I never really reflected on my career choice. I was too busy. Ironically, it is my students, both young and old, who have helped me uncover the elusive answer.

They have become my teachers.

Just recently at a school production, I had a graduate approach me and initiate a heartfelt conversation. Unfortunately, we had to return to the event and were forced to discontinue. The following day I received a message from him that stated, "It's crazy how well you know me, 'cause things aren't going the greatest right now. I know that you picked up on that, unlike anyone else in my life. I think about you all the time and wish we could have talked longer. It would really help." I immediately responded and we made a date to get together.

Who said teachers don't make a difference?

It's unfortunate, we seldom have the time to reflect on our careers, because this vocation is so demanding. We are either prepping for class, grading innumerable papers, downloading our goals for the year, decorating our rooms with learning targets, attending faculty meetings, or perhaps trying to read and meet the demands of the 128-page teacher assessment manual.

And this will not be changing any time soon.

When I did have a bit of free time, away from my busy school day, the last thing I wanted to think about was work. I never had the opportunity to truly reflect on my career and decide whether or not I was making a difference.

Not a moment passed, however, when I didn't thank God for my students. I truly enjoyed hanging out with kids. I *felt* like I was making a difference, but I did not have the time to discover if indeed this was true. (I guess this is what standardized tests are for. We'll get to that later...)

I was too busy teaching—creating important relationships.

Of course, if I could ignore all the distractions, all the government demands and paperwork, I would see the results. My own administration was sensitive enough to allow me to "work my magic," but I still didn't have the time to *see* the results. Luckily though, retirement has allowed me to do this, and I discovered the truth about this noblest of professions.

We do make a difference—from the class valedictorian who sets her sights on Harvard to the struggling student who must work instead of completing her homework.

Teachers truly impact the lives of their students. Because I now have the time to explore this concept, I must perform this much-needed task: *to help current teachers realize that they serve a pivotal role in a child's life.* We stand in line behind Mom and Dad (and at times in front of them) when it comes to our influence on kids. We not only teach them subject matter that is important to succeed, but we teach them about life. We serve as integral role models that capture the important qualities for success: hard work, compassion, love, understanding, and honesty. Let's be real: During their educational years, kids spend more time with teachers than anyone else with the exception of their relatives, hopefully Mom and Dad.

And what they see is often what they become.

Good teachers play a pivotal role in the development of a successful society. Hopefully, they come to realize this, because it's the only thing that will motivate young people to enter this worthwhile profession, and we need effective educators now more than ever. In the midst of all the hate, all the distractions, all the digital mixed messages, kids struggle; they are confused. Students need competent educators who care about them, who can educate them, who give them a sense of self-worth.

A student of mine, Lauren Quintal (2012), has recently become a teacher, and in my portfolio she shares her love of her new occupation.

"I have come to realize how rewarding and wonderful the profession of teaching is, but also how invested and passionate a person has to be in order to develop into a successful teacher. Their heart and soul have to be in it one hundred percent. I am enamored with teaching and absolutely love being a part of my students' lives and learning. If I can be half as kindhearted, vibrant, and encouraging a teacher as you are, then I'll be set."

Lauren truly captures the essence of teaching, even though she just recently graduated with her master's in education. Already, she realizes the influence good teachers have, and *they* must realize it too. With this said, I am dedicating this book to my fellow teachers and all the students of the world who need educators who are passionate, knowledgeable, caring, and dedicated.

So my mission is twofold:

First and foremost, I am dedicating this book to my students. They helped me lead a wonderful life, full of love and laughter, struggle and growth. They have helped me realize how meaningful my profession is, and this in turn has brought joy to my life. Kids deserve teachers who are passionate about kids and truly want to make a difference. By sharing real-life stories, quotes from my "flock" and insights from the classroom, I hope that college students will consider entering the field of education.

We desperately need good teachers.

Equally as important, this book is also dedicated to all of today's educators. It is my hope that I can provide insights, observations, and concrete proof that they do make a profound difference. I want them to feel validated, to continue their good work changing the world. Kids deserve to have educators who can help them make a difference, who can help them make good choices, who can help them figure out the intricacies of life, who can help them attain a meaningful profession. Sound like a lot? It is.

In a self-serving way, I also want society to know that a good educator is a blessing. It is so very important that effective teachers are respected and supported in their mission: to help kids. It's getting increasingly difficult for them to stay focused on their mission, and the support of society is integrally meaningful.

When I began to plan my retirement, writing a book was not on my wish list. In fact, it hadn't even entered my mind until I received my simple yet thoughtful gift. Prior to that point in time, I had made many plans: to hike the Hundred-Mile Wilderness, to raft the Colorado River through the Grand Canyon, and to go on safari in Africa, to name a few. But this unexpected treasure—my three-ringed treasure with the questionable nameplate—reminded me that my job is not done. I can't have my retirement party yet. I must first leave behind the most important gift of all—hope.

CHAPTER 6

That was Then

Teaching has changed dramatically over the past forty years. It is challenging to get past the constraints, the demands, the bad press—all the pressures in today's educational world. Toward the end of my career, I found myself reflecting on my early years teaching and yearning for the good ol' days. There's little doubt in my mind that the new demands of education just get in the way and take the focus off the most important player: kids. It was not that way years ago...

After Lady Luck brought me my first job, I began work at Hodgkins Junior High School, in Augusta, Maine, teaching seventh- and eighth-grade English. (I did start a wrestling program and also coached football at the high school, but we will stick to the classroom for now.) I put in long hours but truly enjoyed the kids. My principal was wonderfully supportive, and the faculty helped the "new kid on the block" with their advice and friendship. It was the perfect learning environment for a 22-year-old, first-year teacher. I believe that this nurturing atmosphere, early in my career, is one of the reasons I developed a love for kids, playing an integral role in their lives.

And we must remember: It's all about kids.

I would like to take this opportunity to empathize with today's teachers, however. Most of my motivation for writing this is to show them that despite everything that is getting in the way, they must not lose sight of the most important lesson plan in education. Its primary goal is to form lasting relationships with students that allow teachers to not only share their "book knowledge" but also to share their life knowledge. We are consummate role models.

This hasn't changed, and never will. Everyone should understand this, from parents, who serve the most important role in children's lives, down to government officials, who are trying to figure out the intricacies of the educational system while often missing the most important ingredient, good teachers.

Oftentimes the whole process gets complicated and confusing. In fact, many times the attempt to improve the system is counterproductive, complicating things that are simple. There are many reasons why today's teachers are distracted. Just look at the system 41 years ago contrasted with today's.

Unlike present teaching challenges, in the past the job of educating these bundles of energy was a joy, uninterrupted by distractions. A typical workday back in the mid 1970s and early 1980s looked very different. I arrived to school at 8:30. (School began at 9:00, because there was usually a parent who stayed at home.) After parking my car, I would leave the keys in the ignition and enter the *front* doorway, even though every door was unlocked. The principal would be standing in the front lobby, welcoming students with his infectious smile. I'd walk to my classroom after visiting the main office to pick up my mail and get an energetic "Good morning, Tom," from the secretary, Barbara Haskell. I might stop at the faculty men's room to make sure that my tie was straight.

During my stroll to my class, I'd visit the teachers' lounge, where many would be smoking cigarettes and making copies of their daily plans on the hand-operated mimeograph machines, the older version of today's copiers. One attractive difference is the old machines used a chemical that, if you inhaled deeply, could either make you sick or get you high. (This may explain why so many teachers had smiles on their faces.)

The loud bell would announce the start of school and students would scurry into class, excited at the beginning of the day and their reunion with friends. My principal strolled down the halls, welcoming them and telling them to have a good day. He returned to the main office while students settled into their homerooms (now referred to as "Advisee Groups"). There were few distractions, with the exception of the morning announcements, which were delivered by the principal over the intercom. Using a welcoming voice, he brought students up to date on the day's activities. Following this, he might either ad lib or remind them of important issues.

My favorite "announcement" was Mr. Wytock's "The Sap Is Running" speech. This reviewed the dress code because the weather was warming and girls would begin to wear clothes that were somewhat "skimpy" by 1980s standards and boys would arrive to school in shorts and tank tops. The speech lasted a couple of minutes, during which he would outline the dress code: no blouses showing cleavage, and no short skirts. No tank tops for boys, and no shorts.

There were few distractions back in the good old days.

The bell would ring announcing first period, and I'd position myself in the hall outside my door to greet my students, who marched into class and sat at their assigned seats. Automatically they opened their notebooks, ready for the day's lesson.

This is similar to today's class, with the exception of the "cell phone effect," where kids are getting to last-minute emails, messages, Facebook updates, and pictures from their friends (and enemies), among other things. Needless to say, their attention is on anything but my subject. So in today's classroom, I must first "entertain" to get students' attention and make certain that cell phones are stored properly.

Undoubtably, the attention span of today's youth is woefully short, unless a teacher can compete with Facebook, Instagram, Instant Messenger, emails, and video games, to mention just a few distractions.

In the "old days," class normally ran smoothly, and if a student acted up he was sent to the office for immediate discipline from the principal, which normally meant an hour detention that day. If a parent had to be involved, most often the blame landed on the student, and he was taken home for retribution, which was far worse than school. A normal conversation if a parent were called would look like this:

Teacher: Good afternoon, this is Mr. Wells calling. May I speak with either Mr. or Mrs. Jones, please?

Mrs. Jones (Mr. Jones is working): This is Mrs. Jones. What can I do for you, Mr. Wells?

Mr. Wells: Well, your son James has not handed in a homework assignment in two weeks. Would you please remind him to do his English homework? We have assignments every night, so you can assume he has one. Please just ask him if he's done it yet, and if not, please work your persuasive abilities.

Mrs. Jones: He hasn't done his homework in two weeks? Are you kidding? Well, I will talk to him when he gets home, and this will definitely not happen again. Thank you so much for calling. Please, next time call me if he misses any assignments at all. I will certainly take care of this.

Mr. Wells: Thanks, Mrs. Jones. I knew that you folks at home would take care of it.

Oh, for the good old days! If, in the event a parent needed to talk to me, I'd get a message in my mailbox from our secretary informing me that

I should call their home phone (the only available form of communication at the time). Overall, it was a respectful process, one that had the student's success in mind, with none of the clutter of today. Teachers now are "available" twenty-four hours a day, by either cell phone, email, texts, Facebook, or Instagram, to name a few.

Years ago, when lunch time arrived, students would congregate in the cafeteria, many eating healthy meals prepared at home by their parents. Talk would be of sports, class, and who's dating whom. Everyone had a forty-minute lunch together, and if students had to go to an activity, they would bring their lunch with them and hang out/eat at their homeroom teacher's room. One big happy family.

At the end of the day, kids either walked to their extracurricular activity or took the bus home, where they would find a supportive parent who asked about their day and provided the love, food, and help they needed. Families would have dinner together, help their children with homework, go to bed, and be ready to do the same thing the following day. At times they would watch TV together, shows such as *Andy of Mayberry, Batman Get Smart, Alvin and the Chipmunks,* or *That '70s Show* just to name a few.

Meanwhile, the faculty would stay at school and busy themselves for the next day's lesson. Oftentimes this would include a visit to one another's rooms to discuss students they had in common and help one another with any problems/issues that had arisen. I recall numerous times when more experienced teachers would pay me a visit, ask me how my day went, and offer friendly advice. I never once felt threatened or judged. In fact, some of my best practices were born out of these conversations. This certainly helped me prepare kids for their next step in life.

After graduating from high school, students either attended an affordable college to work towards advanced degrees or earned a well-paying job at a local manufacturing company. Life was simple then.

In a nutshell schools in the "old days" were far different in the following ways:

- Students were better disciplined.
- Students were more respectful.
- There were fewer distractions:
    - Cell phones
    - Facebook
    - Instagram
    - Instant messenger

- o Video games
- o School shootings
- o "Fake news"
- o Access to misinformation
- There were better paying jobs for high school graduates.
- Society trusted schools. The only standardized test was the SAT.

So, a typical day in today's schools looks far different.

CHAPTER 7

This is Now

Teaching in the Twenty-First Century

The following quote was written by a student of mine who graduated in 2012 as class valedictorian. She eloquently describes what education has become: an attempt by those above to "improve" education by creating standards.

> "Despite the fact that the American educational system tends to create stultifying learning environments that prioritize performance over in-depth comprehension, your clear passion for teaching made learning in your classroom a rewarding challenge that I took pleasure in tackling."
>
> —Nikki Liyagadon

Nikki's observations have proven true. The American educational system has become predominantly performance based, ignoring students' total needs. Yes, there are myriad new "clubs" and organizations attempting to meet those needs, but there is one factor that will continually make a lasting difference in a student's performance, a student's confidence, a student's emotional well-being, a student's happiness.

A good teacher.

Today's new standards, new goals, new assessments have changed the face of education, detracting from the ever-important relationship that's needed to create a happy, successful student. It can have a negative effect, unless a teacher can make good choices and focus on the most important thing in his/her career, *the student sit-*

ting right in front of them, not the proficiency-based standard of the day.

It's so difficult to do this, however, because there are too many distractions. Let's begin by looking at a typical day in today's school.

Before the day begins (7:10 at my school) teachers arrive to finish their prep, grade papers, place learning targets on their boards, download their grades, and check their email for parent correspondence and administrative announcements. For the past thirty years, I have arrived at my high school at 4:30 a.m. I needed the time to prepare, hold writing conferences with students (their record is 5:00) and perform the duties required of today's overwhelmed educators.

Oh, for the good ol' days.

At 6:30 in the cafeteria, students are busily catching up on the local gossip on Facebook, Instagram, and Snapchat, and consequently there's tension galore. Many have their face buried in the screen on their cell phones. Teasing, bullying, gossiping, all keep administrators (and the newly hired police officer) very busy before school even begins. Some students are sent to the office (which now has two assistant principals in charge of discipline), and the rest go to homeroom, now called advisee groups, which is just another responsibility for today's educator.

There, the teacher/advisor takes attendance and reminds the flock that they must meet habits of learning standards by the end of the year in order to graduate.

(These were created by the Common Core, which is based on No Child Left Behind.)

Oh, for the good ol' days.

The principal begins to make the morning announcements. "Good morning, Cony Rams. A reminder that juniors will be taking the science augmentation test this Wednesday in the auditorium. Be sure that you get plenty of sleep and a good breakfast before. Next week there will be an SAT practice session in Mr. Jones's room after school. At the same time seniors will be volunteering at the elementary school. Teachers, don't forget the faculty meeting after school. Please bring your handouts about learning targets and teacher assessment procedure.

"Have a Ramtastic day."

Oh, for the good ol' days!

After homeroom, students walk to class while checking their cell phones for messages, etc., and when they arrive are instructed to put them away. Many groan, and some hide their screens on their laps in order to keep up with the "news." Others ask to go to the bathroom midway through class so they can check their email, Snapchat, Instant Messenger, Twitter, or other social media.

Others are distracted because they haven't had breakfast yet, or perhaps they had to work late in order to help support their family.

While settling in, teachers write their learning target on the board and then announce, "Class, today's learning target is 'Demonstrate a command of the conventions of standard English grammar and usage when reading, writing, and speaking.' Log into your computers and enter the following web address."

It's finally time for class to begin, all the while the focus on the standards that must be met by the end of the week, and the assessments that will define both the students' and teacher's success. Most likely there will be an EdTech in class who is helping a student who has an IEP (Individualized Education Plan). Add to this mixture a number of ESL students (English as a second language) and you have quite the hodgepodge.

I am not downplaying the need to educate everyone. On the contrary, I am supporting the concept that the system should trust teachers to advocate for all students, which is far more effective than any "movement" that I have encountered in my 41 years as an educator. We *will* get the job done. Those who have no experience in education should place their energy elsewhere.

In today's classroom, you have to consider distractions you didn't have in the past, such as a possible lockdown drill, bomb threat, or immediate outburst from a student who just saw herself online doing something embarrassing.

In today's school, during their prep period or lunch, teachers must answer emails from parents, administration, students, or peers. This is in addition to constantly scoring tests, grading papers, writing goals, or trying to meet the government requirement of the day. Their mind is focused on what needs to be done, not how to reach their students.

Unfortunately, that is second on their list. So, do we pay attention to the "system" or to our ever-important students?

Just recently, I attended a seminar at a local college that included students presenting different projects they produced for their education major. Each one of them focused on how to produce lessons that met the standards and requirements. Not one had anything to do with how to be a good teacher. It was totally standards based. I spoke with them afterwards and found out that not one of them had any clue about what it takes to become an effective educator.

They did not realize that they must form positive relationships with their students in order for their lessons to take root.

Today's public schools have students who are far more distracted. I'm not talking social media either. At the end of the day, kids either attend an extracurricular activity (because colleges require them to be "well rounded"), go to work, or go home to an empty house because both parents must work to support the family (that is, if there are two parents living at home).

I cannot imagine growing up in today's world. Technology has provided wonderful innovations to help kids learn, but the flip side of this is access to misinformation, instant gratification syndrome, and distractions galore. I don't really have to elaborate. At this very moment just look around, and if you are in a public place, most all people are on their cell phone. There is no age discrimination when it comes to the dependence on technology.

So, at school after addressing the distraction syndrome, teachers, must go to myriad meetings: IEPs, parent conferences, committee meetings to help organize learning standards, faculty meetings where they discuss current government regulations, or in the lucky event of no meetings they must plan the next day's classes or correct/score innumerable papers. They also have a new responsibility: to prove to the administration that they are doing a good job. This involves pages and pages of paperwork on top of their teaching schedule.

Unlike years past, escaping to their home may not provide respite for today's teachers. Remember, technology has provided access to teachers twenty-four hours a day. Emails, social media, text messages, Facebook (that's all I can name; remember I'm old) all allow instant access to teachers.

Suffice it to say things have changed. There is little doubt that not only has life experienced a shift, but education has as well. Reflecting on my forty-one years in teaching I see that much of the changes in education have been in response to the change in society.

The "traditional" family is a thing of the past. When I first taught, the nuclear family was the norm. The divorce rate was 18% and most kids lived with their original parents. Now, fewer kids live in their "original" home.

There are distractions galore. Technology has provided us with wonderfully efficient ways of accessing information and entertainment. It also affords us the opportunity to communicate instantly. We can reach the masses with the touch of a finger, delivering information in a very timely fashion.

We can gratify our every desire at the blink of an eye.

This has caused great joy, but also created innumerable problems. Let's face it: Most everyone leans on technology each waking moment. At this moment, I am sitting in an airport in Greece (waiting to return from my first major trip following my retirement) and literally everyone is on their cell phones. There's no personal communication, no eye contact, no interaction—no fun.

I do realize that current technology has innumerable benefits, but it has added an element to education that has provided us with challenges.

- The distractions are omnipresent: cell phones, bomb scares, lockdowns, new meetings to learn new requirements, new standards, and new rules.
- Everyone wants things now. Instant gratification (writing process hard).
- There is immediate access to misinformation.

We are currently experiencing the most recent attempt to better our educational system, No Child Left Behind. Despite its laudable goal (to improve education for today's youth) it ignores the most important element:

A good teacher who can form a positive relationship with students.

This makes all the difference in the world, because the truth is this: Society changes, technology changes, and information changes. But when it comes to kids, strip away the exterior and they haven't changed.

In today's world teachers don't have time (or in some cases the knowledge) to create strong relationships with their students; there's simply too much to do above and beyond teaching. There is little doubt that many aspects of the current system are indeed laudable, but many are distracting good teachers and making them feel scared and inferior. This is not the person you want standing in front of a classroom.

Thank goodness I retired when I did—before all the "experts" got involved in education and the assessment of teachers. I know that the key to a successful educational system is its teachers, but by taking away their focus (students) and replacing it with countless new duties, their effectiveness will suffer, not thrive.

This concept became blatantly clear to me when I did something I never thought was on my radar—I returned to school as a substitute teacher. I made this choice not because I needed spending money, not because I had too much free time, not because I needed to boss someone around. It was because I missed kids.

On the first day back while walking through the entrance to my school, I felt a surge of adrenaline. Numerous students excitedly ran up to me with a smile that said, "Welcome back." There were hugs, high fives, and numerous questions about my retirement. Their smiles, their energy, their excitement all said one thing:

"Welcome Home."

CHAPTER 8

Reflections of a Substitute Teacher

"This Is Now" with No Strings Attached

Subbing does not pay well in my school district ($11/hour), but it fills a void that has been created since my retirement, a strong sense of accomplishment. Walking into a classroom brings me joy, and I finally realized an important fact.

I miss the kids—my drug of choice.

It's not that I don't like retirement; I love it. I love the silence; I love sleeping in (well, until 6:30 at least); I love taking walks with my wife, Martha, and my two Corgies, Gracie and Sadie. I love having the time to see my boys, Max and Lucas, enter adulthood. I love it all.

But I miss my students. They too are my family, each and every one of them. So what can I do?

Go back to school—only this time I make my own hours. This time, I work when I want to. This time, I have no preparation and there is little pressure. It's a perfect-case scenario.

There are many reasons I have decided to do this. I have already announced that I miss kids. Unlike many adults I hang with, kids are energetic, positive, and are not constantly stressing out about paying the next bill. I relate to them; I respect them. Most importantly, I enjoy them.

Another benefit is that I get to work on my book, while they work on the "assignment of the day." If I need a quote about teaching, all I have to do is ask the class and I get plenty of feedback. So, here I sit, typing away while I watch "my" students work diligently. I am subbing for a math teacher. Actually, I am not subbing for this math teacher; I am covering for her.

What's the difference?

Well, I have been assigned to sub for a Spanish teacher who has a free period now. Because of the substitute shortage, I have been "asked" to watch another class because they could not find enough subs to cover the day. This is part of today's problem in education—finding substitutes. One reason is the pay, which is not much above minimum wage. Unlike the past when subs were plentiful, most school districts struggle with this. Just another difference between then and now.

But I digress.

I have given my students their assignment and they have settled in. While typing, something just caught my eye: a 182-page book entitled *Teacher Evaluation and Growth Rubric 3.0 Companion Guide.* After thumbing through it, I realize that this is just one of the recent attempts to assess teachers' performance and help them "improve."

One hundred eighty-two pages! It's not just a source to read. It defines all the extra duties a teacher must perform to prove his/her worth. They must reflect on their practices and, after an administrative visit to the classroom, must write about their performance and how it meets standards. Just recently I asked a friend about this, and she said that the principal's last visit resulted in the administrator writing seven pages about the class, while she wrote four. How much time did this take away from her teaching?

I take a thankful deep breath and continue with class.

This is just one of the many changes in education that detract from a teacher's time with students. When I was younger, my performance was judged by the department head or administrator who visited my class occasionally. They would pop in, sit there for a while, take notes, and then leave. Later, I would go to their office and talk about their observations. We would have a productive conversation and highlight the good things going on, and perhaps get some suggestions on how to improve.

This was a positive experience and helped me grow as a teacher. It took very little time and did not detract from my very important duties: connecting with my students, preparing for my class, or grading papers. If I were teaching today, I'd be reading this 182-page book and filling out myriad forms to prove that I am doing my job effectively.

A past student of mine, Taylor Gustin, defines our goals best: Teachers "must take the time to understand their students and not just see them as a group of kids passing through. Teachers must see the potential in all students and also see them as a team. When they rely on one another, so many important life qualities shine through: support, understanding, teamwork, and love."

How can teachers do this when they have to spend their time filling out paperwork? How can teachers form these ever-important relationships when they have to spend each waking moment now satisfying educational "standards"?

I must also mention that just last week, there was a mass school shooting in Florida. Seventeen people were killed, which has prompted the nation to review its gun policy. President Trump has proposed to train teachers to carry weapons and pay them more, like a coaching stipend. Not to belittle the tragedy, but this is another distraction/expectation put on a teacher's plate. We wear myriad hats, so to speak, but in many cases are leaving the most important one at home.

Most educators with whom I talk inform me that they are so stressed to meet the new mandates that they forget their major goal, to form positive relationships with kids so they can/will learn. The most important hat is no longer in the wardrobe.

As a substitute, when I'm in the classroom, I continue to connect with kids, my students for the day. It's energizing; it's positive; it's rewarding; and most importantly it still works.

We must get all educators back on the same page and not let new demands distract them from their duty. My goal is to prove to them that they are making a profound difference and to remind them what it takes to form this ever-important relationship.

Subbing has reinforced everything I believe in and everything I preach: Kids now are no different. You reach them by forming relationships with them, and once this happens, the sky's the limit.

There is no national standard, state law, or educational reform that will work without this important element.

In 2011, The Maine Learning Results were updated "to include Common Core as the college and career readiness standards for English language arts and math, better preparing our students for success in college, career, and civic life by creating deeper, more rigorous, and clearer expectations for learning."

Sounds impressive, but without connecting with kids first, without making them feel valued, without forming this all-important relationship, *nothing will work*; it's all for naught. It's not easy, but it's definitely worth every minute.

CHAPTER 9

A Kid Is a Kid Is a Kid

I am absolutely certain that in the past forty-one years, at the base level, kids' needs have not changed—at all. It became blatantly clear to me just recently, after I retired and returned to teach one last writing class. It is this group that highlighted the importance of forming strong bonds with our students

I study my classroom full of students who are busy working on a research paper that is supposed to argue a controversial topic. The end of the semester is one week away, and they are scrambling to either "catch up," or maintain their high average, or just "get by." It is now that I realize that every class I have taught over the past forty years is the same: filled with kids from different backgrounds, each with his or her own needs.

It's a relatively small group of students—sixteen to be exact. They are part of a new experiment called the Bridge Program, which is an opportunity for them to earn college credit while taking a class in high school. Part of the requirements is that they must take a class at our local technical school (Capital Area Technical Center) and while doing so are offered college-level classes in English, math, science, and social studies. The local university (The University of Maine at Augusta) provides the credits, and teachers must earn certification.

So what I see before me is a hodgepodge of kids, all from different backgrounds, each with different needs (just like any other class). What makes this different is many of them have never been challenged like this before, signing up for "easy" classes and just making it with as little work as possible. Most are intelligent; some are motivated; others think they can succeed with little work.

In my classroom, they have discovered it a tad different.

What I see is a typical group, even though it's not "supposed" to be. They are kids; they have families; they have friends; they have needs. They want to be accepted, respected, and successful. It may not look that way, but this is the reality of teaching. This is our job. The challenge is we must first connect with each one in order to help them succeed. We must find a way to show them we care; we must respect them; we must bond with them. It's only then that we can teach them.

And this hasn't changed.

Proof of this can be found in a letter written by a student whom I taught in 1986 and also coached in wrestling. Marc Levesque thanked me for believing in him, for respecting him, and for showing a genuine interest in him.

He thanked me for doing this for his son as well, thirty years later.

At the same time, his son, Andrew, thanked me for the same things. Students are human, and the human psyche does not change. Despite the decade, kids need the same thing in order to be successful and happy. Marc (1986) proves this in his letter.

It is curious how many things in life come full circle; take for example how thirty years ago I was a privileged to have Tom Wells as my English teacher during my senior year. Fast forward to present day and now my son is also fortunate enough to have Mr. Wells. To think that he has had such a profound role in my son's development as a writer, mentor, and as a person has taken me back to the impact that Tom Wells had on me all those years ago.

My first experience was with "Coach" Wells. He was my wrestling coach as a freshman in 1982. I had no experience wrestling, and I was lanky and relatively weak. I signed up for wrestling as a way to assimilate and gain friends at Cony. I came from a very small and relatively sheltered Catholic school, so Cony seemed huge and intimidating. Upon showing up to wrestling practice, Coach Wells made it a point to inquire about our personalities and discover nuggets about our other interests and activities. In so doing, he discovered that I also belonged to the Capitol City Rifle Club. From that point forward, I was nicknamed "Pistol."

Trust me when I say that I did not fit the nickname, based either on my physical or my wrestling abilities, but it was a cool nickname, and it made me feel like one of the guys, and for that little act, I was eternally grateful.

He continued to push me in practices to improve my conditioning and techniques, all of which were huge confidence boosters for a young man trying to find his way in life. I won only a single wrestling match, but it was so meaningful because it allowed me to find success in something that was outside my comfort zone.

I also had Tom Wells as my English teacher my senior year. Mr. Wells had a reputation as a tough educator with lofty expectations. What I found to be true was that if I provided consistent effort I was able to meet his expectations. I received a solid foundation in writing that has continued to serve me well throughout my lifetime.

Mr. Wells, thank you for connecting with, and leaving a lasting impact on, both me and my son. You have provided us with lifelong skills that go way beyond the ability to compose a proper sentence. The confidence in our own abilities that you fostered with your ability to put people in situations in which they can succeed is deeply appreciated. Those are the intangible skills that cannot be easily stripped away. Very few people have had the opportunity to have had the same teacher as their offspring and been impacted as powerfully.

Thank you from the bottom of my heart. Hopefully, you can attack retirement with the same gusto as you did your teaching career."

Good Luck,
Marc Levesque

Marc eloquently captures the needs of kids in 1986 and also the qualities of an effective educator. Guess what? Kids haven't changed. Teaching is still all about relationships.

So, if kids haven't changed, then reason would dictate that their needs haven't either. Teachers must remember that despite all the IEPs, learning targets, performance standards, and government interference, they have the power to help kids, and this is through forming meaningful relationships with their students.

Another student who was a member of this class captures how important this is. Mackenzie was struggling with a number of issues, and

I made special amends for her in class. I allowed her to write in the empty hallway, so she could focus and not get distracted by the other students, with whom she felt uncomfortable.

She truly appreciated this. "You also helped me with a lot of family issues whether you know it or not. Being allowed to write something about my childhood and what I went through without being judged made all the difference. It is a huge deal to me. I became more confident and began to realize that I am a worthwhile person. This is more important than anything I learned in school. Now I can graduate knowing that I will be successful."

Without knowing it, I was forming a relationship that addressed Mackenzie's needs and ended up giving her enough confidence to not only finish the class, but also win a prestigious writing contest, along with $1,000 cash. *This did not meet any national standards or learning objectives*; they take care of themselves if you form positive relationships with students.

It's imperative that we, as educators, understand what it takes to do this, because there is little doubt that it works better than any national edict from above. Through the use of my "portfolio," students have taught me what it takes to become the most effective educator possible, and we all want that, don't we?

CHAPTER 10

Breathe Deeply and Focus

Before I begin my exploration of how to create strong relationships with kids (according to kids), I must continue to discuss the complications in today's schools that distract us from focusing on what's important. We must understand that we chose teaching as our profession not because of the high salary, but because of the return: making a difference in a kid's life. Yes, it's more difficult than before, but it's worth it.

Let's simplify the problem. Our educational system has undergone a huge transition, much of it caused by a number of factors: technology (both good and bad), the increase of the single parent home, poverty, immigration, violence, cell phones, social media, and the confusions created by mixed media messages. Most importantly, we now educate a greater percentage of the current population for greater periods of time. This often includes a high percentage of students for whom English is their second language. All these challenges have led to numerous attempts to improve our educational system.

Let's face it; we live in a completely different world now.

With that said, this has put pressure on schools to improve their "performance." Unfortunately, this has led to an increase in government involvement, and people who have never worked in a school are making decisions for us. There's little doubt that many "experts" are making sound decisions, but most are data-driven, not teacher-driven, not student-driven. It's a fact that standardized tests do not measure the most important factor of all in a person's success, *a strong value system and a healthy respect for oneself and others.*

Student/school performance is a laudable goal, but how do we measure it? Does a standardized test capture learning performance? Is it a test that captures information a student learns, or does it illustrate in-depth understanding? Should this be the only area for which a school receives a "grade"? Can we compare/contrast test results between schools with high socioeconomic strata with that of one that has a high poverty level?

Does an institution address all students' needs? Does it have a gay/straight alliance? Effective Special Education Department? A safe environment with an officer on duty? Programs that address the countless needs of all students? A math team? A unified basketball team for disabled? A strong ESL program? It's complicated.

That's my point.

Administrators have a difficult job, trying to meet standards while keeping teachers feeling validated. They have parents, school boards, the media, all yearning for an "A" school, while the reality is they might not have an "A" population. I'm not saying that all kids can't learn; it's just that schools have varying starting points, so to speak. Additionally, no one will argue that some kids have far more "distractions" than those students that come from a family with two parents who help them and become a partner with the local school. It's like a sports team; you may have kids who are not athletic, but you work toward improvement, not necessarily a championship season.

It's a balancing act. Teachers must feel like they are performing well, and it is the administration's job to fairly assess them and help them grow. It's difficult to accomplish this with all the "requirements" in today's educational world. The most recent 128-page teacher assessment manual is a laudable goal indeed, but add this responsibility to an already overworked faculty and the end result is anger, frustration, and *decreased* performance. It is the administration that must monitor this, and their workload is rather full as well. Assessing teacher performance has become a business, not a partnership.

Teachers and administrators have a considerably increased workload, mandated by the government, with no increase in pay. This is depressing and unfair, but not the worst part.

It negatively impacts students.

If teachers must perform more work in the same amount of time, something has to give, and that something is their performance in the classroom. They have either the time to create relationships or tweak lesson plans and follow the mandate of the day. Feeling stressed and unappreciated, they do enough to get by; oftentimes the losers are their students.

How can they teach with joy, meaning, and passion when the only thing on the educator's mind is the next learning target, standardized test, or performance indicator? How can they remain positive in the classroom when they are stressed to the max?

In today's educational atmosphere, it is so easy to get caught up in all the new laws and requirements and forget about the most important element for true success in the classroom, forming relationships with kids.

And if we do this, as a team we will accomplish wonderful things. Heather Towt, a student I befriended back in 1998, captures this well. "I'm so thankful that my friends and I were able to get such a great education in a public school setting—more unique these days, especially where I live (Chicago). You were a fantastic group who prepared us so well for college and beyond. You cared about us, so we cared about ourselves. This made us productive and happy."

We can't let *anything* get in the way of what's most important in education, forming positive, loving relationships with students. When we accomplish this, we will be protected from all the confusion. After all, if our students believe in us, if they know we care about them, if they know we love our subject matter, they will mold into successful adults, and everyone is happy. We are then protected from the meaningless administrative attempts to prove to everyone that we are doing our jobs.

Graduate Veronica Swain captures this concept effectively. She astutely observed that good teachers had their own agendas, because they were getting results, and the community was happy and believed in them. She observed, "But Wells always seemed kind of invincible in the face of the system. He could bend the rules because he was protected—partially by his indispensable knowledge and experience, but mostly by love.

"His students absolutely loved him."

As a team (faculty) if we show kids we care, that we believe, that we are excited about what we do, then the sky's the limit. Together, we can make a huge difference, unimpeded by outside interference.

After all, one of the most successful businessmen in America, Steve Gates, knows that teachers who can connect with kids can accomplish educational success. Cony graduate Nicole Liyange-Don writes of Gates, "In addition, he has testified before Congress on several occasions in his crusade to fix our broken system. Gates was recently asked what single aspect of the public education system he would instantaneously change if he were given a magic wand. His response? Hire the best teachers."

There is a formula to achieve teaching success. It's giving students what they need, and an effective educator accomplishes this. And more.

CHAPTER 11

Love Your Students

S o, how do teachers reach students? What qualities must they possess in order to help kids, in order to educate kids, in order to make a difference in their lives?

The answer is found in my portfolio, *The Educational Bible According to Students*. By sharing their valuable insights, kids have supplied me with the answers. It is their own words that have allowed me define the most important "laws of the classroom."

Just recently I was contacted by a student whom I had a number of years ago. Katie informed me that she had just been hired to teach English, and she was both excited and apprehensive. I told her that I'd be glad to mentor her, and she replied, "Thank you, Mr. Wells. I couldn't have done it without you setting such a great example in school of how inspiring it is to be an English teacher. You proved that it takes not only knowledge of your subject, but knowledge of kids as well. Thank you so much. Hopefully we can get together for a cup of coffee and I can pick your brain!"

I am certain that Katie's students will feel valued, just by the way she teaches.

In my portfolio, my past students have also validated an educational career that affected each and every one of them. Ben Lucas, class of 2014 shares, "You were a great mentor, teacher, friend, and an even better person. We have tons of memories that will last me a lifetime, and ones I will never forget. Thank you for making my high school experience such a positive one, and thank you for having such a big impact on my life. I couldn't have asked for a better mentor or role model."

So, how do we accomplish this? The answer really is quite simple: We must forge a connection with our students. Once we forge this bond, our kiddos will do anything to please us, and the end result is growth—educationally, socially, and morally.

According to a fellow teacher, Bruce Baker, a recently retired teacher at CATC (Capital Area Technical Center), kids are his "drug of choice." This perfectly encapsulates how teachers should view their student. They should love them; they should respect them; they should look forward to each and every moment spent with them.

And students sense this.

This is true, now more than ever. It took me eight months to finish reading my "portfolio" because my students wrote with passion, with truth, and with honesty. After taking the time to finish reading their eloquent insights and digest what they said, I've arrived at the following "teaching lesson plan."

Love your students
Love your subject
Love yourself

Believe in your students
Believe in your subject
Believe in yourself

Exercise humor
Exercise humanness
Exercise honesty

Model and set high expectations
Model strict discipline
Model selflessness

Show your passion
Show your caring
Show your energy

Celebrate their successes
Celebrate your successes
Celebrate your school

According to their views, it's as simple as this. No matter what grade/subject you teach, if you follow this model, you will connect with your students and they will reach their goals and become better human beings along the way.

This is true now more than ever.

Teachers must believe that they play an integral role in their students' lives. They can't expect to have their kids tell them, but it happens. Larry Dingus, a very troubled teen I had back in the early 1980s shared, "At the time I wrestled for you, I had no idea that what you were teaching me would be helpful in life. It allowed me to become successful, even though at the time I did not appreciate it. Thanks so much."

No teacher can be successful without relating to kids. This can only be accomplished by being as well rounded as possible. It's imperative that we know what makes our "clients" tick and then tap into their passion. Whether it's sports, music, drama, or playing video games, we as teachers must demonstrate to our students that we understand them and can relate to them. There's little doubt that my involvement in all the activities while growing up allowed me to "speak their language." My enthusiastic conversations with my students proved to them that I cared.

This is not to say that all teachers have to have participated in endless activities in order to relate to kids. They just have to learn enough about their students to show an interest in their audience. This makes kids feel wanted.

When this happens, we form a strong bond that is irreplaceable. When we form this connection, there is nothing we cannot accomplish.

Dylan Cheever, class of 2012, eloquently captures this important bond. "Those late nights in your room at CATC were where I learned what it meant to build something that I could be proud of, to the last painstaking detail, regardless of recognition or success. It was simply about investing in something worth creating and spending our time together to make it a reality. I never felt closer to anyone, and it changed my life. The more you put in, the more I got out."

So what qualities ensure that teachers will reach their students?

Most importantly, a teacher must genuinely like kids and believe in their abilities. I realize it's unrealistic to think that all kids are intellectually capable of mastering the complexities of all subjects, but every student has the ability to perform. It is their right to have someone help them reach their potential, not only in the subject, but in life as well.

My own students support this. Many, in their letters, focused on the very important relationship we form, based on my caring about them. Without this, it's a tough sell. Our students must know that we believe in them, and that we would do anything to help them succeed.

One student of mine, Abby Tardiff, class of 2010, penned a note that captures this eloquently. "High school is a tricky time for students and you always had your door open to them all. It didn't matter if you had them in class or not, all Cony students knew that if they needed a place where they were valued, it was room 2004."

As a matter of fact, I actually created a place in my classroom for all students to hang out during their lunch break. I designed my own "living room" and invited all to come to room 2004 if they needed a place to study, visit, nap, or just hang out with their friends, away from the overcrowded, busy cafeteria (food court).

Why did I do this? Well, I had both an altruistic and a selfish motive. On one hand, I knew that in the cafeteria, there was chaos, groups of cliques that were not always kind to one another, kids yelling and screaming—not necessarily a relaxing atmosphere. It was not a bad or dangerous place, but like all school cafeterias, it did represent a place where some students felt out of place.

Because I was lucky enough to have a huge classroom (which used to be part of the vocational school and served as a graphic arts room) I had space enough to bring in a beanbag chair, a lounge chair, a couple of standard chairs, plus a bookshelf that housed many popular novels. After making it available to kids during lunch, it became fairly popular, housing anywhere from a couple of kids to as many as a dozen per day. This forced me to stay in my room during lunch, but that was my norm anyway, to work during lunch, and we were one big happy family.

It is there that I built strong relationships with all kinds of students. I would eavesdrop on their conversations and give advice when needed. I also learned about the issues that were troubling kids of the time so I could connect with them. It was a wonderful way to build trust, understanding, and relationships that allowed me to help them with school and other challenges they had. They all felt valued in this setting.

The key word here is *valued*. No matter the year, no matter the age, no matter the circumstances, everyone wants to feel a sense of self-worth. This makes them want to please the person (teacher) who values them. Not only do they produce because of this, they grow emotionally as well.

When I became department head at my high school, I immediately assigned myself the lowest level English class (after a strong "suggestion" from my principal). I have described this class earlier, in my narrative about Billy, which explained my use of the word "dumbass" and how my portfolio received its title (Chapter 1). They were an interesting mix of freshmen, none of whom were overachievers. But by the end of the semester, we were a team, and each one of them felt good about themselves and one another. It was because they knew I cared.

I had a senior helper for that class, Taylor Gustin, and she noted, "Teachers must take the time to understand their students and not just see them as a group of kids passing through. Teachers must see the potential in all kids and also see them as a team. When they rely on one another, so many important life qualities shine through: support, understanding, teamwork, and love."

It doesn't take a rocket scientist to know that each and every human being wants to be liked. They want to feel valued. Kids are no exception; in fact, it is more important to them than any other age. They are new to the world, they have little confidence, and the most important thing to them is having others like them, no matter how hard this is at times. I did not learn this fact in my college education courses, but I do know that I love kids, and they know this.

And it works.

Taylor noticed this in my classroom. In her goodbye she also stated, "Your job was not to grade scholarly essays, but to have compassion and understanding for kids who truly needed it. And they needed you in the worst way. I saw them change; I saw them grow; I saw them to start to believe in their abilities. And this was all because you loved them."

Realistically, sometimes it's hard to love them, but our actions must show them we care. This need is universal and will never change, and a note I received from a parent proves this. I taught Kate Levesque back in 1986, and her insights capture the fact that the need to be loved is not only timeless but must be part of your lesson plan. She states, "It takes intelligence, skill, patience, and talent to teach high school students English, but it takes heart to *care* about your students as people. Thank you so much for caring about Andrew; it means more than you know to him and to us. It made all the difference."

If your students know you care, then they want to please you. It's the perfect time to move to your next lesson plan for successful teaching:

Set high expectations.

CHAPTER 12

Set the Bar High

"I used to take every moment for granted and half-ass my way through everything. After taking your class, I can't even fathom how ignorant that is. I've never worked so hard and felt so good. For that I want to thank you and tell you how much I appreciate your dedication to teaching."

—Molly Silsby

The most common theme in my retirement portfolio is students thanking me for "kicking their butt." If you love them, and they know it, they want to please you. They push forward, work hard, and want to meet your expectations. It's hard to believe at times, especially with tougher students who hide their feelings and challenge everything you do. But there is little doubt that the secret to successful teaching after creating a loving environment is simple.

Set the bar high.

Early in my career, without even realizing it, I demanded a lot from my students. Despite the fact that my career started teaching junior high school, I still expected my students to perform up to their abilities, and beyond in some cases. It doesn't matter what the grade, human beings love the feeling of working hard and finding success.

Just recently I reflected on this. Why did I find this the right thing to do? I really hadn't learned this in college, but it just seemed appropriate. When I finally looked in the mirror, I saw someone who had high expectations. Granted, this was not always true, but after years in high school getting decent grades with as little work as possible—and a couple of years in college with the same attitude—I finally grew up. Interestingly, I feel that athletics played a major role in my growth.

You see, I always participated in sports. I'm not saying that they are the answer in all cases, but they taught me that the harder I worked, the better I got. I could see the results, most times fairly quickly. A three-sport athlete for eight years (high school and college), I improved because I never let up (probably as a result of competing with six siblings while growing up).

And I loved the feeling of success.

I'd have to assume that most teachers work diligently at what they love. They can relate to hard work and realize its benefits. Hard work yields success, and in turn this creates feelings of euphoria that at times are addictive. With this in mind, we can apply it to our own students, knowing that eventually they will appreciate the results of dedication and focus.

And good teachers model this as well.

My own students resoundingly support this concept. The vast majority shared their appreciation for making them work harder than ever. From gifted students to those who struggle academically, this theme held true. Caitlyn Snow was a very intelligent student with some personal issues who hadn't been challenged for a long time. In my portfolio she writes, "I wanted to say thank you for kicking my ass this past year. It's rare to come across a teacher that actually cares about his students. Most just give deadlines, and if it's not done, then too bad. But you do anything and everything to help us succeed and get the best grade possible. You make it challenging, but it feels good when I'm done. Thanks for caring."

You'd expect this epiphany from a class valedictorian, but not also the class clown, the class "dummy," the class jock, or the class "laziest person alive." To a T, they all thanked me for challenging them.

The lesson they learn is that hard work is satisfying, even though the journey may be frustrating. The harder you make them work—and they try because they want to please you—the better they feel when they have accomplished their mission. Because I forged loving, positive relationships with the majority of my students, they didn't want to disappoint me—or more importantly themselves.

Lexi Lloyd, class of 2016, was a good student, but also another one who got by on as little work as possible. She learned not only that hard work feels more rewarding, but also that it pleases others, and she liked the feeling. "I don't think I have ever been pushed as hard as I was in your class. You had high expectations, and when I knew my work wouldn't meet them, I worked until it did.

"Sometimes, I hated you for that, especially at midnight when I was writing that insufferable Obama State of the Union rhetorical analysis. But in the end, it felt damned good."

Brettany MacFarland, class of 2014, agrees. "I hope we can live up to your expectations, because no student wants to disappoint you."

Corey Lim, class of 2011, also liked the challenge. "I've always appreciated your 'no bullshit' approach. You are never one to tread lightly and have helped many students, including myself, kick the fluffy writing style that we were attuned to. High school is known for being a confusing and significant time in one's life, and I will always appreciate the level of realness you delivered to us daily."

This does not always make you the most popular teacher, at the moment at least. I found it difficult knowing that my expectations were creating intense anxiety in my students. But it's like parenting—You must believe that in the end everyone benefits. It will help your students grow, mature, and achieve a sense of fulfillment.

Taylor Gustin (the teacher helper I mentioned earlier) was a talented student, and she knew it. She liked receiving good grades with as little work as possible, but this changed in her junior year. In my class, despite the fact that she was a good writer, she struggled early on, but worked diligently to improve. She became one of my favorites, because she truly realized the importance of challenge. In her reflection she writes, "You definitely knocked my ego down a few notches, which is something I needed. My writing improved as did my confidence, and for that I am eternally grateful. It is a life lesson I will never forget."

Challenging students can be difficult, especially when they have different capabilities and strengths. It's important to try to get to know them and adjust your expectations accordingly. In today's educational world, this is difficult. Treating students as individuals has been replaced by standardized testing. Common Core is a system that holds all students to the same standards. This is truly a laudable goal, but it's totally unrealistic—and more importantly unfair.

With this concept in mind, how do we "level the playing field"? How do we help all students succeed?

They must know that we care about them. They must know that we will set high expectations, *but realistic ones*. And then they must know that we love our subject and have the capability of making them love it too.

It's called passion.

CHAPTER 13

Love Your Subject

So, what exactly is passion? It's hard to define, especially when it comes to education. Teachers must have a love affair with their subject. Some lucky ones have a deep fondness for their area of interest prior to their careers, but then there are some who develop it slowly, but surely.

I fall into that category.

As evidenced in my "biography" in Chapter 4, thanks to my parents, I liked to read when I was young, but never truly cared about writing or English for that matter. When it came to choosing a subject for which to receive my teaching certification, it came down to the lesser of many evils. Yes, I liked English, but I also liked math and science as well. In fact, I began my college career as a pre-med student.

The point is that I did not enter the teaching field with a true love for my subject. It grew slowly, but surely, and has developed into a craving—if you will—for each and every one of my students to appreciate our language and all its power. I get more excited over finding the perfect word than the perfect piece of chocolate.

This love affair with English has allowed me to reach more students. Behind caring for my kiddos (which is proven by my high expectations), loving my subject is vitally important. Hundreds of kids have commented that they did not really like English prior to entering my class, but by the end of the year, my addiction became their addiction.

One student captures it eloquently. Olivia Deeves (2014) makes the connection between my passion, my expectations, and the positive effect it has on my students. She writes, "Something about your passion and love for writing made me want to try harder and take in every bit of information you would give me. As you assigned home-work, I found myself excited to get started and prove myself."

Rebecca Sproul (2014) also feels that this passion can be a game-changer.

She has aspired to become a teacher and reflects on qualities that affected her.

"Your passion for education and for your students has inspired me in my own career path. Although my plans are not exactly the same as yours once were, the way that you conducted yourself as an educator will forever impact my own teaching style. I hope that I can fill my students' minds with laughter, passion, and confidence, just as you did for me."

Robert Swain (2012) was an intelligent member of my horde, and he noticed the role of passion in teaching as well. "When I was in high school, it didn't take me long to figure out that I was learning English like never before, but it wasn't until after I had graduated that I understood why. The time and effort you put into your job is truly admirable, but your passion and expertise are what set you apart. Your love for education is infectious—you don't just teach; you make kids want to learn."

Because I have this passion, I truly enjoy planning my classes. I want my audience to love English the way I do. At times, I'd invent things to get them interested. Whether it's putting a word of the day on the board and rewarding students with candy for the proper definition or having pizza parties for a class that performed well on an essay, it was always fun and enthusiastic.

Rebecca Sproul continues to capture the importance of loving your subject. "Thank you for being enjoyable, engaging, entertaining, eccentric, encouraging, and most importantly—enthusiastic. That has been the biggest thing for me. Your energy made me want to continue to turn in papers better than the last, and work harder than ever before. I know teachers aren't thanked nearly enough for all they do, but on behalf of all your students—thank you."

A concrete example of my passion and how it works is my writing conferences. Instead of marking up a rough draft and returning it to my student (who then copies my suggestions without learning much) I require everyone to register for a minimum of one meeting with me to review the paper they are writing. At said meeting, the student must read his/her paper aloud while I listen. Prior to their recitation, I ask the following questions:

- What is your topic?
- What is the goal (purpose) of your paper?
- Who is your audience?
- How do you accomplish your goal (paper's plan)?

The student then proceeds to read to me, while mulling over the questions. This takes time and hard work, but it truly helps them become better writers. Our conversations are lively, emotional, and inspirational. Not one student leaves without feeling a sense of accomplishment because he has lived in the shadows of Wells's passion.

The initial requirement of a writing conference is they must register for different time slots during the day and must appear on time. In fact, my writing conferences begin at 5:00 a.m. and most times are not part of the class period. I have even had students show up for conferences on snow days, when, unbeknownst to them, school has been cancelled!

And the point is, they appreciate it. They adopt my passion and feel a sense of self-worth. Robbie Buck and Amelia Trudo, class of 2015, capture it well. "Whenever we sit down to write anything, whether it be a research paper or a text message, we hear your voice in our heads telling us that less is more or that we need to trust ourselves and that any risk we take will indeed pay off. The early morning writing conferences were hard to get to, but they energized us and allowed us to personally adopt your passion for writing. You have become an echo in our minds and will always be someone to look up to."

Passion for your subject comes in many forms; it doesn't have to take the form of some excited teacher running around in front of students. It doesn't have to be loud; it doesn't have to present itself in any one form. I've been accused of being overly enthusiastic at times. I do get a tad flamboyant, but it works for me.

We all have different ways of showing students that we care about our material. They know when you love your subject. Just recently I had a colleague share with me her insights that support this.

Laurie, fellow English teacher and "producer" of my "Dumbass Portfolio," is wildly successful. Students love her and look forward to learning in her class. While visiting her last week, she confessed that when I was a fellow teacher, she had some resentment towards me, not because she believed that I was a very successful teacher but because she thought that in order to prove to her students that she cared deeply for them and her subject, she had to run around and perform for them—like me! This was truly surprising, because if anything, I was jealous of her and the success she had with students.

The point is we all have different ways to show students that we care about them, and truly love our subject. Laurie's quiet demeanor, subtle sense of humor, and kind/compassionate façade all made students feel important, feel comfortable, feel wanted, and feel like they wanted to please her and love her subject like she did. **You don't have to teach like a pirate** to prove to kids that you are passionate about your material.

I think that elementary school educators must have it tough: They teach all subjects and must show their students that all subjects are important. In this case, passion still plays a major role in connecting with students and helping them learn. At this level making a connection with their students and showing them that all subjects are important is a laudable goal, and their caring relationship will help them accomplish this. Their passion for *learning* will then become quite clear to their students. Youngsters sense it, even at that age. It's then that the sky's the limit.

In high school, it's the love of our subject that drives us to connect with our audience. We will do anything to get our students excited. There is one assignment that pops into my head that supports this theory accurately, and it definitely wasn't part of my lesson plan originally. My passion for kids and writing came through once again.

I was introducing a rather challenging assignment one day, and it was obvious that my students were somewhat disinterested. Most were not planning on college, and I was asking them to write personal narratives, which can be challenging. The major feedback was, "This is so boring. I have nothing to write about. My life is boring, just like this assignment."

Of course, I did not take this personally (a very important trait to have as a teacher). But then Lady Luck entered my classroom. While I was running around trying to excite my yawning students, a young man in the center row shouted out, "What happened to your finger?"

Looking down, I noticed that my hand was close to his face, and my missing fingertip was somewhat obvious. At that moment, I had an epiphany, and replied, "I'll make a deal with all of you. I will write a narrative about how I lost the tip of my finger. I will read it to the entire class in two weeks, on the day your final drafts are due. This will only happen if everyone in class does their homework every night, hands in their papers on time, and has a minimum of one writing conference. Two weeks from today."

There rose a rumble of discontent, but they agreed. Following that day, I began each class with a countdown. "OK, everyone, take out your homework. If every one of you has finished it, you are (fill in the blank) days away from hearing me read 'The Saga of the Missing Fingertip.' You won't be disappointed."

Following that, I began class with a lesson in writing and then we proceeded to edit each other's narrative and work diligently on different drafts. At the end of the class I would announce the homework assignment, which was always followed by my students motivating each other to get it done and threatening those who normally would not do their homework (a positive spin on peer pressure). Sometimes, if I felt that they were losing interest, I would add a tidbit from my narrative. Some of my favorites were, "It has to do with a dog that was hungry," or, "There were a 1976 Volkswagen Beetle and a slow-moving teacher involved with my missing finger as well."

Two weeks flew by, and when I collected their final drafts we would celebrate by enjoying "The Missing Finger and the Hungry Dog" story, and most years, it was accompanied by assorted tasty treats my students conspired to bring in.

And this all happened because I have a passion for my subject and my students. I would do *anything* to help them learn. I suppose creativity played a role in this story (and my teaching) as well.

Perhaps the most concrete proof and highest compliment came from a fellow educator, who recently shared his shrewd insights with me. Robert Lippert (B.L.) was a student of mine (Class of 2000) but now serves as a friend and fellow educator. He is a gifted teacher and coach. His retirement message to me captures the role that passion plays in the arena of education.

Your passion and energy are infectious and worthy of emulation. You've raised the bar for teachers in this district and established a standard of excellence that is very difficult to match. However, even if we try and fail in our efforts to duplicate your profound impact, there is one group that will benefit regardless: our students. And to me, that's the greatest legacy you can leave. Students you never had or maybe even never knew received a better education because of you, all because of your passion.

If you love your students and love your subject, your students love your subject. Humor doesn't hurt either!

CHAPTER 14

Laugh a Lot

"Not only were you good at making sure students understood everything, but also if they didn't, you'd find some humor that would make it understandable for kids like me (special thinkers). You helped the kids that really needed it."

—Zach Dionne, class of 2016

You don't have to be funny to be an effective teacher, but in my case it helped. My students made it abundantly clear that my sense of humor helped them get through some trying times and even helped them learn my subject matter.

Kids relate to compassion; kids relate to understanding; kids relate to acceptance. It's all part of the equation. Humor, at times, helps promote many of these qualities.

There are many student "character types." The majority, I have found in my case, like to laugh and appreciate a sense of humor. It relaxes them, puts them at ease, and helps them learn. Initially, class of 2016 valedictorian Molly Silsby was not impressed by my sense of humor. She "hated [my] dumb jokes and occasional crudeness, but now it's one of the reasons [she] will miss [me] most of all."

As far back as 1986 humor helped me connect. At that point in time, I had a student, Dianne Gousse, who had just had a huge fight with her boyfriend. She arrived in my room, tears flowing freely, sobbing uncontrollably. Immediately I asked her what was wrong. She informed me that her boyfriend was being mean to her, and that she did not know what to do.

I placed my hand on her shoulder, looked into her eyes, and told her that I was sorry about her circumstances. With confidence, I told her that I had the solution to her problem. She looked up at me hopefully and asked me what it was.

"Wait here and compose yourself; I will be right back."

I left her sitting comfortably in my room and exited. A few minutes later I returned, walked up to her slowly with my hands behind my back, and said, "I think I know what we can do to make you feel better and forget about Robert."

She looked up at me with hopeful eyes and asked, "It's so hard for me. What can you do to make it better? He's being so mean to me."

Slowly, I pulled my hands from behind my back. She gasped, and then laughed out loud. Giggling hysterically, she asked, "Where did you get those boxing gloves?"

I replied, "It doesn't matter where I got them. What does matter is how I am going to use them." Her boyfriend then magically appeared in the doorway.

"Look who's here, right on schedule," I chided. "So, Robert, I hear that you are not treating your honey with the respect she deserves." Pounding the gloves together I added, "It's time for an apology."

Dianne turned toward the doorway and laughed out loud, and spontaneously the unhappiness and tension in the room disappeared. Robert, visibly relaxed, apologized for the way he was treating her. For some strange reason, this may have put things in perspective for her. Perhaps in today's toxic environment I would not have done this, but way back then, it seemed the right thing to do.

In my portfolio, Dianne herself reflects on the incident. "I remember I was all upset fighting with my boyfriend; he was being mean to me. We went in to see you during recess so you could help us work things out. You came walking in with some boxing gloves and asked if they would help. We all laughed out loud and everything was better. Of all the things I remember, your sense of humor was the best."

My need to lighten situations for my students so they could put things in perspective has been appreciated by many throughout my career. It keeps things light while I am asking them to work like they never have before. I am known as one of the toughest teachers at my school, and students remember this. But what else they remember is that the tough learning was fun. They then make the association that learning is fun.

Let my students tell you:

"Your natural sense of humor and energetic teaching style put me at ease and had me far more engaged than any other class. Hell, you could have been talking about something as boring as grass and I would have been hanging on your every word, along with the rest of the class."

—Olivia Deeves, 2014

"You have a talent for making writing enjoyable, even at 6 a.m. You were always hilarious, picking on the football players (when they didn't even know it) and making fun of everything you could."

—Riley Hopkins, 2014

"There are so many quirky things about you that I am going to miss: your humor, your love of betting with students, the way you work out obsessively."

—Zoe Barlowe, 2013

If you are comfortable with it, keep it light; students learn well this way. If this does not coincide with who you are, then be true to yourself. *Kids can spot an imposter a mile away.*

Do believe, though, that the most important characteristic you should exemplify is to believe in yourself—know that you are making a huge difference in your students' lives. Have confidence in your love of students, love of subject, and the rest will take care of itself.

CHAPTER 15

Trust Yourself and Good Things Happen

My students have defined the qualities needed to reach them, and when teachers are sensitive to their needs, kids can't help but grow into productive adults.

Eventually.

Of course it may take some longer than others, but it happens. With little doubt, if we treat kids with respect, with admiration, with love, and with acceptance, they have the best chance to not only succeed, but to be happy with themselves and their lives.

Realistically, there are obstacles that may prove challenging, but when we graduate kids who are accepting of others, who like themselves, who believe in themselves, and have received the education they deserve, success is inevitable.

Knowledge alone is not the key; it's just a part of the puzzle of life.

I have shared stories with you that offer proof, but it also comes from beyond my retirement "Dumbass Portfolio." I continue to hear from adults about my influence on them and the role I played in helping them figure out the mysteries of life and how to find happiness.

Just a few weeks before I wrote this, a student whom I coached in 1980 connected with me on Facebook. He posted "Today is my 30th anniversary clean and sober. So grateful that it's just another day."

I congratulated him, and he replied spontaneously. He said that he had just posted something about me in a local Augusta Facebook page and he wanted to share it with me. It was a video of him wrestling at Madison Square Garden in the late '80s, winning his weight division. He wrote, "I wanted to send this to you years ago, but I never got around to it; booze got in my way. I know you'd be proud of me, but being sober is something more important to me. I wanted to let you know that you played a huge role in my life when I had you as a coach. You accepted me, even though I was a bit different. I didn't know then that I was gay, but I had suspicions. You showed me that all people are valuable, and that hard work and acceptance are two of the most important qualities that a person can possess. Through these lessons, and your support at a difficult time in my life, I can say I am happy, and fulfilled, and much of this has to do with you."

As usual, my throat tightened and my eyes misted over, and I felt grateful that Lady Luck helped me become an educator. I do want to reiterate, however, that I am not unique; all good educators have the same impact on their students. *This book is not about Tom Wells; it's about all productive teachers.* They must realize that their *job* is the most important of all. We help kids with life, with love, with their own personal happiness.

Many donations to the "Dumbass Portfolio" allude to the power of a good education, and more importantly, the power of a gifted educator. I've chosen some of my favorites that capture my life-changing role. We all help students in our own way, and **my students' comments can apply to any caring educator.**

It's a no-brainer (as evidenced in the next chapter) that as a *team* of caring educators, we make a profound impact on our kids. If you are a teacher, please read the following quotes aloud, while picturing one of your students delivering it.

If not, read and enjoy. Perhaps you might consider becoming a teacher, or at least get online and thank them for their role in your life, or your kids'.

Students Say It Best

"I wanted to say thank you for everything you have done for me, and if I were ever given the opportunity to do it over again, then I would be much better, and it is all because of you. I wanted to let you know this because you are an awesome teacher and an even better person."

—Mackenzie Stephenson, 2017

"I always made my best attempt to channel any available energy into your class. On the days that I could get out of bed, your class was the one I tried to work in."

—Jonas Long, 2017

"I thought being successful meant the world would know your name, you would have your own Wikipedia page, your name would be in the news. Yet here you are, a teacher in a tiny unknown state. You'll never make world news, someone from California won't recognize you, but nonetheless, you are just as successful as anyone will ever be. This is because success isn't measured in how well known you are or how much money you earn. Success is measured in your ability to positively impact others, in your dedication, persistence, and hard work.

"I hope that one day I can be like you. If I could even be half the person you are, I would consider myself blessed. I am so proud to have been your student. Any compliment on my writing is a compliment to you too, because you have truly shaped my writing to what it is today, and for that and more, I will be eternally grateful."

—Molly Silsby, 2016

"Now, for the sappy part. This letter goes beyond thanking you for teaching me. It's for helping me through the rest of high school. It's for listening to me when I complained about my senior English class. It's for telling me to suck it up and to try to work with him, but still helping me edit my papers. It's for offering to kick Justin's butt after we broke up and for all the advice that helped me get through that difficult time. It's for always being straight up with me, especially when I needed it.

"It's for caring."

—Lexi Lloyd, 2016

"One thing we can both agree on is that there is no forgetting you. You'll forever be a mentor and friend to us, and thousands of others.

"We know that one of your favorite expressions (used when we complain too much) is, 'Life sucks and then you die,' but after having had you as a teacher and friend, we must modify it to, 'Life doesn't suck, and then you die.'"

—Robbie Buck and Amelia Trudo, 2015

"I want to be articulate and eloquent in my ode to you, but I am finding it incredibly difficult. There is so much I want to say to you, Tom Wells, and so much I want to thank you for. Mr. Wells, thank you for everything you taught me about writing, life, loss, and acceptance. You have played an influential role in creating the strong woman I am today, and I can never, ever thank you enough."

—Taylor Gustin, 2015

"Though I only had you as a teacher one time, you pushed me to be a better person and work hard for what I want. These simple lessons have carried me through college and through life with a better understanding of myself and the world around me."

—Olivia Deeves, 2014

"Overall, you have poured more passion and knowledge into being a teacher, mentor, coach, and role model than any other teacher or professor I've encountered. I can't thank you enough for being such a large part of my life."

—Riley Hopkins, 2014

"High school is a time of tumult for many, of turmoil for some, and I suppose that is where my thanks begin. I believed in very little then, least of all myself. My thoughts and emotions seemed foreign, even hostile; my writing, I felt, odd and frequently ill fitting with enthusiasm and integrity. You inspired me to embrace my oddness, to use the darkness that suffocated me as fuel for my art rather than allowing it to be a hindrance.

At a time in my life and education when so many sought to tell me what to think, feel, or do, you treated me and my peers as adults, capable of rational, intelligent thought, who needed only guidance. You showed rather than told us how to use our perspective to broaden our worlds, not to narrow them. As simple as it is, your ability to see us as humans, worthy of compassion and respect, meant—means—the world to me."

—Nikita Aube, 2014

"I really hope you realize how much you meant to each and every student you ever had. We all loved your sense of humor, your turn of phrase."

I just want you to know that my first book (or Oscar, because that's gonna happen) will be dedicated to you. I may not have been the best research-paper writer, and I may not have survived all the "Wellsonian" rubrics completely unscathed, but I do believe that you're proud of me.

And now I can die happily."

—Emily Simonton, 2013

"Where do I begin? To say that you've influenced my life is an understatement. Hopefully I'll end up somewhere I can influence at least one person the way you've influenced me."

—Meaghan Jellison, 2013

"...but you are and always will be one of the most influential individuals I have come across in my life. You have provided me with another "guy" that I can talk to about anything and someone that I can just have a down-to-earth conversation with. In a way, you remind me of myself."

—Sam Hopkins, 2013

"You're one of the most influential people in my life."

—Zoe Barlowe, 2013

"I feel as though I got to not only consider you a truly great mentor, but a friend as well. What nobody else really knew was that you arrived to school at 5 a.m. every day. They didn't know how late you stayed after the bell had rung and the busses had gone. They didn't know how keenly aware you were of how the building was running. They didn't know how personally you saved kids who were teetering on the edge of troubled, dead-end lives as sixteen- and seventeen-year-olds and influenced them to make more of themselves than their circumstances could allow. It wasn't about recognition or personal gain. It was about investing in something worth creating and spending time with people—your students."

—Dylan Cheever, 2012

"Finally, let me say thank you for everything you did for me in school. I've never had a professor so willing to sit down with *every* student in their class with the sole goal of helping them improve. You are the best and most memorable teacher I've ever had, and I have a feeling you've touched so many lives in more ways than you realize. Congratulations on your retirement."

—Bret LaForge, 2011

"Mr. Wells, I have tried and tried again to write you a letter that at the end would have you in tears. I don't have the words. I wanted so badly to be the one to break you down. I don't know why; you've just had a major impact on my life and as I've gone through my adventures, I've always thought of you. You've been a guide for me even when you weren't right there.

"I think you'd be proud of where I am in my life these days. I credit my mother, beautiful women, myself, and you for this.

"I hope to enjoy life the way you have: to fall in love with a wonderful woman, to raise my children by being the best father I can, to always smile and laugh, and to encourage others and show them that each day of life is an adventure You are a good man."

—Chris Scot, 2010

"Here we sit in our little condo almost seven years out of high school (and by we, I mean I am sitting here at the kitchen table typing this heartfelt letter, while Chris is watching the Top 10 Video Moments of *Trailer Park Boys*) wondering what to say to our high school English teacher as he ends his career. What to say in just a few words what his class, his expertise, and his mentoring did for us?"

—Holly Parker and Chris Logan, 2009

"You have been a force in the Cony community, and there are so many who are grateful for your contributions as a coach, mentor, teacher, and friend. You were the reason I kept up with my classmates at Bowdoin, both on the track and in the class-room. You were also the reason why I held my head up high after melting onto the hallway floor into a sobbing heap, heaving just learned that I was denied acceptance to the fifth of five colleges to which I had applied. You said this would seem like the worst day of my life, but that one day I would look back and say that this was the most rewarding challenge. You told me that this would be character building.

"It was. Thank you."

—Anna Ackerman, 2007

"I also can't write a letter of reflection without mentioning Chizzle Wizzle and all the fun we had. You were hands down the best interlocutor ever (with the best minstrel cast, of course)! I remember one night there was a small issue and I lost the mustache I was wearing. It was Thursday and they were taping the show for TV. I was a tad bemused. In typical Wells fashion, however, you said something like, 'What the heck are you upset about. That was the best show ever.' I think of that often, too. And it helps me remember to look at the big picture and focus on the positive."

—Brian Berger, 2006

"You taught me so many things during high school. You taught me how to write, how to edit, how to be critical of my own work, how to be critical of other students' work, but most importantly you taught me to be a whole person."

—Meaghan Stiman, 2006

"It would be an understatement to call you one of the best teachers at Cony. I still draw from things I learned in your class and on your team. I learned how to challenge myself in reading, writing, and running and most importantly, I learned how to continue to strive to do them better."

—Sophie Cook, 2002

"It may surprise you that these memories are so vivid for me, some twenty years later. I, however, am not surprised—you were a gifted teacher, and a memorable one. Having teachers like you ultimately inspired me to teach, as well. After an unsatisfying stint as a corporate lawyer, I returned to school to complete a PhD in Literature at Vanderbilt! I'm submitting my dissertation this week, and ultimately I will be a professor of 19th-century American Literature. Thank you for being part of that journey"

—Faith Barter, 1997

"Ever since I learned of your imminent retirement, I've spoken with several classmates and teammates about the profound impact you had on all of us. We have all gone on to do many things with our lives; we are lawyers, doctors, teachers, journalists, accountants, scientists, parents, and everything in between. We all, across the board, attribute much of our professional and personal success to the profound gift of your teacher and/or coaching."

—Melissa (Mansir) Stelberg, 1997

"And today, because he, Tom Wells, my mentor, not only gave me knowledge and passion as a student, but also gave me the support as a teacher to become the educator I am today!

"Cheers to you, Mr. Wells! I am the educator I am because you were my teacher, my mentor, and most importantly, my friend. Thank you, Tom, for all you have done to make a difference in the lives of so many."

—Carrie Anne Lasselle, 1986

"I know it sounds dumb, but I was never one to make any sense. Sorry I let both of you down, but I need time to think and to get my life together, and when I do that, maybe I'll come back, but if I don't I want you and Mr. Albert to know that I love you both very much. Thank you both for everything you have ever done for me."

—Larry Dingus, 1982

"But even after all that I learned from you, I still can't express how tremendously grateful I am that our paths crossed—because I know you changed the direction of mine forever."

—Natalie Hallak, 2011

If you are an educator, these are *your* students talking. Not everyone is going to love you, however. No teacher connects with all students.

That's why we have a faculty: a group of educators who love kids, who love their subject, who believe in their profession, and most importantly, who believe in kids. Together, they strive to make certain that no student is left behind.

It's called a team.

CHAPTER 16

The Most Important Team of All

Kids have many needs, and it is difficult for all teachers to fill each one of them. Some can accomplish this, but not many, and that's OK. It is imperative, however, that students get the attention that they need and deserve. With this in mind, schools hire teachers who know their subject matter but also know how to reach kids. We all have our strengths and must exercise them in order that all students get the education they deserve, academically, emotionally, spiritually, and socially.

There's no *I* in team. It takes a village to raise a child. (Pardon the clichés) The bottom line (another cliché) is that schools are teams of teachers, run by the coach (administrator). We all have our role to play, and when we have to, we "take one for the team." (I'm done with my sappy clichés.)

One of my students said it best in her "senior goodbye." This is a writing assignment given by our very talented English teacher, Laurie Rodrigue, during which the student must choose at least one person in his/her educational career and thank them. Some students moan and groan and pen a cursory thank-you, but the majority write from the bottom of their hearts, and often to more than one teacher. The next chapter will develop this idea. But for now, let's experience the team effort captured by one very eloquent student.

Victoria Emery, class of 2014, masterfully illustrates how a team of high school staff helped her develop into the successful young women she is. Her senior goodbye is entitled "Goodbye, Au Revoir, Hej Då." She indeed proves that as a team, teachers and support staff will provide the mentorship, advice, guidance, and education that kids need to lead a happy, healthy life. In her Goodbye, she reflects:

One. Simple. Word.

Yet, it seems to be the worst word in the world…unless it's for a short time. But, the point of goodbye is to move on, start a new chapter in your life, and thank the people who were there for you in the past so you can continue with the present and move to the future.

"Remember me and smile, for it's better to forget than to remember and cry."

—Dr. Seuss

"I love you more than songs can say, but I can't keep running after yester…"

—John Mayer

"Be the change you wish to see in the world."

—Gandhi

There is an incredible amount of people worthy of thanking during my high school career. People who helped me through the hardest of times, made me laugh when I needed it, and the people responsible for making me learn a life lesson.

The teachers I had throughout the years were wonderful in helping me with the curriculum, but also showed me how to grow up. I have a long list, so bear with me.

I must start out with my 8th grade homeroom (and science teacher), **Mrs. Chounaird**. Easily enough, you taught me how to ORGANIZE.

Generally, I'm a messy person and I don't always organize my binders, but I keep myself on-track by writing lists and keeping things in labeled folders thanks to you. You were always very adamant about keeping us organized, so here's me coming back to say thank you. It helped a lot in high school and I hope I can carry those skills to college.

Next, **Mrs. Marston**: I hope Mrs. Rodrigue is able to deliver this to you because you were my very first homeroom teacher. You taught me a lot: how to make substitutions if you didn't have all ingredients for a recipe, as well as how to deal with life issues and drama. You were always there as my shoulder to cry on. Coming in to get tea and eat lunch with some friends was great too. Thanks to you as well for being understanding about my tardies and letting me "student instruct" your class instead of actually getting detention. (Shhh. I won't tell if you don't!) You're a woman who tells it like it is and won't take crap from anyone. You have a heart of gold, and I wish you well in the rest of your cooking travels in life. Thank you.

Mrs. Carpenter: When I met you for the first time, you were the great new French teacher "Madame Weston" at Lincoln Elementary School. I remember thinking it was going to be a fun class. I never really got the hang of French, but you tried to make it fun with colorful projects and songs to help memorize…regardless of if it was "standard practice" for French vocabulary. I still sing, "Lundi, Mardi, Mercredi, Jeudi, Vendredi, Samedi, Dimanch…" And now, looking back, you had such a beautiful voice, and I remember thinking, "I wish I could sing like that." This year I tried out for the elite musical group at Cony, the Madrigals, and I got in…so thanks for getting me into singing and making me realize it's actually a fun de-stressing exercise, which comes in handy all too often. You understood that kids weren't going to learn if the lesson wasn't fun.

Speaking of Madrigals, I'd like to say a big thank-you to **Mrs. Beaudoin**. I was scared entering your classroom to try out for this prestigious group. I had never really sung in front of one person before, but now I was faced with a roomful of people. It was the scariest moment of my life. You asked me to match pitch with some notes on the piano, then let me choose my favorite song: "Fix a Heart," by Demi Lovato. After my voice broke in the first few notes, you kindly asked me to start over. I nailed the notes at the climax of the song, and I was the happiest girl in the world.

For the next week I was biting my nails, waiting for the list to be posted of the next lucky group to be called the Madrigals. You FINALLY posted the list and when I saw my name, tears came to my eyes. I truly loved my experience in the Madrigals, and I can honestly say much of this was due to the fact that you made us feel special. You cared about us more than any teacher I have ever had.

I have no words to describe what you did for me over the past year. From gaining confidence and helping me get over my stage fright, to getting me to test my boundaries and try new things. For all this, I am eternally grateful.

To another music-woman in my life, **Mrs. Sleeper**, I owe a debt of gratitude. When you first arrived at Cony my junior year, I could tell that you wanted to make great music with us. You were the first band teacher to get emotional with us, showing us your human side. You were always so caring, treating the band like family. If anything were ever wrong, you'd always be there to listen. I felt like you were there when nobody else was.

Speaking of loving teachers, I must thank **Mr. Dostie**. I don't know exactly why, but I always loved the immense amount of sarcasm in your class, because I appreciated that you'd tell a student that they're stupid when they were actually being stupid. You always called it like it is, which is something kids need: honesty. I think I got along with you the best, just because we understood that there ARE stupid people out there, and most of them are just acting that way. They need someone who calls their bluff, and you're the man to do it.

The next in my teacher-family lineup is **Mrs. Dale**. You are the most adorable and funny teacher ever. Science was never my strong suit, but you gave us permission to tell each other to "move your fatty acid" when they got in the way. You also taught me how to use note cards, which I still do to this day. It's the only way for me to learn something thoroughly. For my new life skill, and making me smile on the days that seemed unbearable, I thank you.

This brings me to **Mr. Braun**, always cheery and happy. I'm hon*est to* God telling you the truth that if you were a stranger, and I passed you in the street, I would not think you were over forty! So, good job being the healthiest person in Disgusta (that's Augusta in case you didn't know). Your love of superheroes was always something I could connect with. Funny, I didn't meet you when you were a health teacher, but as my gym teacher when I was a chunky little kid in elementary school. You were the most fun gym teacher I ever had. And I kind of followed you…err, maybe the other way around…through the years in middle school and high school. I changed from a chunky kid, to a girl with decent eating habits, which helped me get to a healthy weight. And I thank you for that, because

I pushed myself to get healthier and now I feel great. You gave me the gift of health.

I'm not going to lie, the most boring class goes to US History and Civics…with **Mr. Cooper**. Despite this, I loved your humor and the fact that the only cookies you ate were chocolate chip, which I could bake and earn "cookie points" that did not hurt my average. I appreciate your understanding and forgiveness of my "homework disorder" and your pushing me harder and harder so I could earn a good grade in your class. Despite the fact I found your class sleep inducing, I learned a lot, and it seemed like every one did, because you accept each student for what she is—no judgment. You're a badass on that motorcycle as well.

Your next-door neighbor, **Mr. Millet** is my next target. You are so incredibly passionate about your work because you love it. You make your students understand it, with multiple venues. Your excitement and creativity made learning fun, and for that, I thank you. As my swim coach, you pushed me and made me set goals for myself. Now, I love to swim and every time I'm in the pool it feels natural and effortless. It has helped me stay healthy as well.

Teachers who pushed me and were brutally honest? I can thank **Mr. Wells** for that one. I'm sure that if someone were to analyze the rhetoric in this paper, I would be hearing some laughable comments. I never really got the hang of rhetorical analysis, but despite this, I feel that I am a much better writer now. And I have Mr. Wells, the King of Dumbasses, to thank. I remember when I wrote what I believed to be an epic essay on his test, only to find out that I misread the question and didn't even answer it. I recall the comment on the paper: "Well written essay, Victoria. Too bad it doesn't answer the question, you dumbass! See me about a rewrite." And now I love to write, and I have you to thank. You weren't afraid to treat us like the adults you believed us to be, and I appreciate that. I developed my character in your class, so thank you. I love you, Older Dumbass.

Last and definitely not least, a huge shout out to **Mrs. Rodrigue**. There's little doubt that my teachers have helped me become the person I am, but during my senior year you provided me with a role model that to this day I emulate. You represent everything that is good in mankind, and I have you to thank for so many things. You helped me through the bad grades I kept getting in your class, and helped me turn my 65 into an 88. But I must share with you, the most pivotal moment, and one that represented for me what it is to be a good person:

I had been having a miserable day, and apparently you were the only one who cared enough to notice. I was sitting in your class, minding my own business, and when the bell rang, everyone sprinted out, while I took my time. You sauntered over, looked me in the eye, and asked, "Is everything OK, hon?" I wasn't prepared for this act of kindness, so without looking into your eyes, I replied, "I'm fine," and I proceeded towards the door. You then said, "It's OK, you don't have to tell me," to which I replied, "You're a very perceptive woman." I headed toward the door (even though you were standing in front of it) and you took me into a warm, loving embrace, and told me everything will be all right.

I cannot describe in any words how that made me feel. I'd never had anyone care about me that much. It was honestly the nicest thing ANYONE has EVER done for me. I thought about that small scene while I drove away from school that day, and bawled my eyes out the whole way. You are the most caring teacher I have ever known. I love you and hope you never change. I will never forget you.

I will miss my educational experience in Augusta. I feel that each and every person has influenced me and helped me grow into the person I am today. I even miss the little things: the art room where I could express my feelings; Keith Stockmar, the singing janitor who was always nice to everyone; the nurses who never doubted me when I was sick; and the YMCA pool, where I felt safe, nurtured, and healthy.

This letter exemplifies my point: We, as a team, mold kids into the adults they become. We all "own" a piece of them, and help them become happy, healthy, and whole.

What other occupation can make this claim?

CHAPTER 17

Senior Goodbyes

The Way Life Should Be...and Is

Question: What does an English teacher do with her seniors who are about ready to graduate? What will motivate them to write? What will motivate them to think? What will motivate them to invest themselves?

The answer: senior goodbyes. Yes, you already read one in the previous chapter, but there's more to it.

According to its inventor, Laurie Rodrigue, this assignment turned out to be a class favorite. What initially started as an *attempt* to keep seniors interested and focused, turned out to become their favorite writing assignment. This says a lot considering the fact that seniors about to graduate typically represent a group of lazy, whining teens that are ready for the next step in their lives, and this doesn't include putting forth effort in class and staying focused.

With this in mind, Laurie created what turned out to be a winning assignment: Their instructions?

"Choose your favorite teacher(s) and say goodbye to them. If you do not have a favorite teacher, choose a place. This assignment may come in the form of a narrative, an expository piece, a poem—anything that captures your insights and feelings regarding the role this teacher/place has played in your life."

To me, this represented a fascinating, meaningful assignment, one that prompted me to visit her recently to gather further information. After initial hellos and hugs, I asked her for some background to her senior goodbyes. Laurie shared with me. "This assignment took me by surprise. After moaning and groaning, which seniors do quite well, they began to reflect on their years in public education. All of a sudden they are turning to their classmates and telling stories and sharing memories. Before I knew it, they were busy writing, trying to capture the powerful effect teachers had on their lives. I didn't predict this, but it was truly empowering for both students and teachers. They eagerly passed them in on the due date, waiting for feedback."

After grading and rewrites, students were instructed to staple their masterpieces onto a piece of colored paper that held the inscription "Senior Goodbyes." After that, the fun began.

At the end of the school day, after teachers left for home, students would stealthily walk to their "victim's" room, look both ways to see if the coast was clear and tape the senior goodbye to the door or wall outside the entrance, then sneak away. They all loved this part. The goal was for the teacher to arrive the next day and be greeted by senior goodbyes scattered all over their door and outside wall.

Each year, I looked forward to that day. In fact, most of my fellow educators felt the same. We were all transported back to our youth, hoping that when we arrived at school, we would be greeted by these wonderful messages. Some teachers receive their goodbyes early in the week, and others not until Friday, or at times, the next week. It didn't matter; they always brought joy and meaning to our lives.

And ironically, seniors looked forward to this challenging assignment. It held true meaning to them.

This writing piece turned out to be a truly powerful and fulfilling experience for teachers and students alike. What better way to both validate our careers while at the same time teach kids the importance of reflection and appreciation? This exercise genuinely captured the life-changing effect good educators have on their students.

Now for the bad news. She introduced this assignment about eight years ago and continued it for six years. Recently she discontinued it for a number of reasons. She doesn't teach every senior, so some teachers were left out. Additionally, with the arrival of Common Core, its standards, its teacher assessments, and its omnipresent paperwork, this particular assignment did not appear to be "meeting the standard."

So this meaningful, powerful learning experience met its demise, much to the chagrin of both students and teachers alike.

On my recent visit I felt a tad guilty to bother her. I knew that she was buried in work, but when I mentioned this assignment, she lit up and sprinted to the back of her classroom. Stopping in front of a filing cabinet, she grabbed the handle on the second drawer and pulled it excitedly. Inside lay hundreds of sheets of paper, each and every one filled with meaningful words. Most were stapled together and attached to a piece of colored construction paper that bore the title at the top: "Senior Goodbye."

Laurie shared, almost apologetically, "This is not all of them, but I retrieved the ones left behind. I just couldn't throw them away. They are just too moving to toss into the trash."

"How many are there?" I asked, impressed with the mound of papers in front of me.

"I counted them a long time ago, so I'm not sure. I think at least a few hundred. But this is just a small sample of them anyway."

Grabbing the "goodbye" at the top of the pile, I noticed the name, Chandler Shostak, which happened to belong to a previous student of mine. He was a cocky jock who thought too much of himself. I remembered him vividly, also because I coached his dad on the football team about forty years ago. I decided to read it, not expecting much, but I got far more than I asked for. He vividly captured the concept that a team of good educators changed his life.

Since the first day I walked into Cony High School as a smart-ass, punk freshman, I knew it was going to be a special place. In actuality, I underestimated how special it was going to be. Cony has been the scene of so much positive growth in my life; it's crazy to think of how much I have changed in these last four years. I have developed athletically, academically, and personally, and Cony has been there for it all. It is an exceptional place to be, and I wouldn't have wanted to spend the last four years of my life anywhere else. My personal growth is a testament to the wonderful student body and the friendly, easygoing teachers and coaches.

I came to Cony as a little bit of a troublemaker with an attitude. I probably talked back too much and disregarded the rules too often. Proof of this would be my school record. I received more detentions my freshman year than I did the remaining three years combined. This is because I was immature and misguided, but fortunately I learned quickly. The teachers here taught me how to grow up and follow the rules. Mr. Wells and Mr. Dostie were a couple of the first teachers I had, and I rapidly found out they wouldn't put up with any bull. I learned that if I wanted to be respected, I would have to give them respect as well.

My football coaches also taught me important lessons. They taught me how to make better decisions. I learned if I was going to play on a high school team and be a remotely good athlete, I would have to be aware of the little eyes looking up to me and watching my every move. I would have to make smarter choices and hold myself to a higher standard. I couldn't get into trouble at school or be doing the wrong things outside, because my team was depending on me and the community was watching.

I've made spectacular friends here, some that will be lifelong. I have made awesome connections and have memories that will last a lifetime as well. Because of the connections I've made and the experiences I have had at Cony, I will not be like many students at other schools who are ready to get out and never look back. Cony has been great to me, and I have enjoyed almost every moment (with the exception of freshman year).

It has helped me reach my peak as an athlete as well, and I know when I go to college I start at square one. I'm not sure if I am ready to leave yet and take one step closer to a boring adult life, while looking back on "the good old days." I'm hesitant to leave all of the good times and great friends and teachers I've met here. Cony is a huge part of who I am and I'm a little uncertain of what lies ahead.

Ultimately, I admit I'm not completely grown up yet, but that's more than OK, because I never expected to be at this point. I'm still human and I don't always make the best choices, but that's adolescence and I tend to take all the good times I can get. Cony has helped me to grow up, however, and I realize that I have the skill set to become a successful adult and, more importantly, a happy one. I thank Mr. Anastasio, Mrs. Buxton, Coach Dostie, my guidance counselor Mr. Hinds, Coach Lip, Scorin' Morin, Mr. Poulin, Mrs. Rodrigue, Mr. Totman, Mrs.

Tripp, Coach Vach, and Mr. Wells for helping me get here and bringing me a giant step closer to who I want to be."

Thanks for all you guys do,
Chandler Shostak

When I finished reading Chandler's senior goodbye, I paused and reflected. I always liked him, but I thought that he felt entitled and was a tad condescending. It felt rewarding to know that our educational *team* had accomplished its goal: to help him become a young adult who realizes that life is a big classroom and that we are always learning how to become better human beings.

I looked again at the pile sitting in front of me, filled with hundreds of senior goodbyes. The first paper I grabbed turned out to be so powerful that I needed more. Like a drug addict looking for his next fix, I reached for the second paper in the pile, hoping that it would be written by a student who had Mr. Wells for a teacher.

Bingo.

"So Long, Farewell, Auf Wiedersehen, Goodbye"
By Emily Simonton

I can't believe it's time to do this. Ever since I was a freshman and saw these senior goodbye papers being posted everywhere, I was excited to be writing my own in three years—but also dreading it as well. It doesn't seem like it's time for me to be saying goodbye to all the amazing people I've been around for a good chunk of my life.

It hasn't sunk in yet.

If you asked anyone who knows me, the first word they'd use to describe me wouldn't be "overachiever." (A vast amount of my friends are overachievers, but not me!) However, sometimes it happens. I go all out when I feel like it. And because my teachers played such an integral role in my life and development as a human being....

I feel like it now.

Mrs. Fylstra: At first, you were just my integrated science teacher. Personally, I've never really enjoyed science, but I had a great time in that class. You were a caring teacher who made it fun. But once first semester was over, I rarely saw you. And then at the beginning of sophomore year, I was sitting in the food court before school started, and you came up to me and asked how my summer went. I really appreciated that because I knew, sadly, I wouldn't have a class with you that year.

Mr. Dostie: (I know you're not a teacher anymore. You've gone to the other side: administration!) I hate math. I honestly do. I'm awful at it and I do hate it. But I always looked forward to going to your geometry class—go figure. I will admit it; you scared the bejesus out of me at first. Your whole "If you do something stupid, I will make fun of you because you deserve it" speech freaked me out. But somehow we forged a bond. A girl who doesn't go out or her way to watch sports, a girl who was a member of the band, and a girl who enjoys English above anything else, I was mystified. But I don't care. I have so many great memories of your class.

I also want to mention how much I cherish your love of the pep band, which is my pride and joy. Every time I hear you whistling "Land of 1,000 Dances" around school, it brings a smile to my face because that's my favorite song.

Mr. Lippert: Yet another football coach I've had as a teacher, I was so afraid you were going to hate me. I'm not too interested in government or politics—well, certain aspects of them—I don't really care about football, and I was extremely intimidated at first.

But I ended up loving your class.

I don't know how, but it's one of my favorites. You wouldn't let me write rhetorically. You talk during our quizzes and tests. You're all about football and the height/weight stats and "no word banks on the vocab tests." I honestly should hate you, but I don't (Boom! Roasted).

You're funny, engaging, you appreciate my humor. Heck, you even said that I was the best writer, which absolutely means the world to me. I had a great time in your class and I'll miss you a lot.

[Please note all of the rhetoric I'm using right now. See how you have deprived me all year long?]

Mr. Braun: I first met you when I was eight years old. You were the cool, new gym teacher at Lincoln Elementary School and everyone loved you.

When you were with us, you also taught at the Flat Iron building. I was sad to be leaving you at the end of the sixth grade, but—surprise, surprise—you wound up teaching phys-ed at Hodgkins Middle School. So I got two extra years to geek out with you and tell you what the "song of the day" was. In eighth grade, I came up to you and jokingly accused you of stalking me and said that you were going to follow me to high school next. You laughed and told me you weren't going to be teaching at Cony. Guess you were wrong about that!

I was really sad when I found out I wouldn't be having you as a teacher anymore. So, every chance I got, I'd slip into your room and talk to you. Over the ten years we'd known each other, we've bonded over Big Brother, '80s music, Harry Potter, Batman, other comic book characters, Tom Hardy as Bane. The list goes on!

I'll miss you so much when I'm at college next year, but I'll make sure I come back and visit you as much as I possibly can because, like I've said all year, you are the muscular, physically active, baldheaded, male version of me.

Mrs. Beaudoin: I've only had you for two years, but they've both been amazing. If I had a time machine, I'd go back to one of the last days of eighth grade, when Mr. Hinds came into my social studies class and made us sign up for high school courses. I'd somehow turn myself invisible and "accidentally" nudge the frumpy fourteen-year-old's hand so she would cross off chorus. Of course, Middle School Emily would know that she didn't mean to do that, but maybe she'd reconsider. And if that would fail, I'd just come to her at night when she was sleeping and whisper in her ear Jiminy Cricket style. Either way, I would end up in your class. If you don't understand what I just wrote, that's OK, because I'm not sure I do either.

All right, enough with this ridiculous scenario. I just want to say how much fun I ended up having junior year, when I finally ended up in your chorus. We went to Williamsburg, which was a great trip, although I found out my grandfather had passed away during it. I was crying my eyes out before chorus competition and you gave me the biggest hug, and that meant so much to me. I will never forget it. Even though I was bawling, you convinced me to still get up there and sing, and dedicate it to my grandmother. I did so, and I could see you smiling at me throughout the concert, and then once we were done and leaving the stage, you squeezed my shoulder and told me that you were proud of me. I will never forget that.

OK, I'm trying not to cry now. Um…happy thoughts… Oh! The prestigious Rammy I was awarded this year was awesome; I seriously love it. The fact that I'm the first (and only) winner (for now) also means the world to me. I was overjoyed to be recognized in front of the whole school for my love and dedication to music. Thank you so much for everything.

Mr. Scarpone: I know that you are teaching in Brunswick now, but I'm hoping that Mrs. Rodrigue can deliver this to you. I just want to say thank you for inspiring me to stay in band all of these years. It's been really rewarding and a lot more fun than I let on.

When I first heard about you, I'm not gonna lie, I was like, "What the heck kind of name is Scarpone?" (Remember, this was fifth grade!) Anyway, I'd heard glowing remarks from my brother about you and how awesome you *are*. I'd already decided I was going to join the band—mostly because my brother was doing it—but once I heard the legend of "The Scarp," I knew I'd remain in the band for a long time.

I must admit, I was pissed that you left my freshman year; I felt betrayed, but I realized that it was a necessary move on your part. After you left, however, everything I played, every song I sang, I dedicated to you. When I play I still see you sitting right there in the front row watching me and giving me confidence.

Thank you so much; you were an inspiration and true friend.

Mrs. Sleeper: In four years, you were my third and final band instructor. I can't say how much this year's band has meant to me. You revitalized us. You took a group of talented teenage musicians and made us sound professional.

I hope you enjoyed the seniors giving you a gift during our last concert. There's no band seniors manual that says we have to pool our money and buy you a gift, but you certainly deserved everything we gave you and more.

You're the sweetest teacher I've ever met. Thank you for letting me stay in your room during lunch. Thank you for your support. Thank you for all the meaningful conversations we've had.

I love you more than you'll ever know. I can't wait for our get-togethers with Michelle down the road!

Ms. Tripp: Mama Bear Tripp! I love you sooooooooooooooooo much! You are hilarious, kind, compassionate, amazing.... Words can't describe how much fun I have in your classes—even though you accuse me of having an inappropriate crush on a certain person I definitely do not have a crush on.

When I was younger, I'd heard about you from my brother, and I knew that I'd be in for a treat when I took honors global freshman year. And I was.

Our relationship started when I wrote our first assignment. I can't remember what it was about, but I kind of wrote mine with an extremist point of view. You mentioned it to the class and thus created confident-turned-somewhat-annoying-Emily.

We just get to one another. We're both easily amused. We're both funny. We're both interested in psychology. We're both visually impaired. We're both girls. We both have noses...I mean, we were meant to be.

But seriously, I could just walk into your class, having the worst day in the world, and I would immediately feel ten times better. You give off this great vibe, and I can't be upset (which is almost impossible for a teen)!

You are one of the most caring teachers I have ever had. I have watched Mama Bear in action. You go to the end of the earth for any and all of your students. I haven't needed you to do anything for me (yet), but just knowing that you'd have my back means the world to me.

I can't explain just how much I love you. I love sitting and talking to you about everything and nothing. You don't judge people. You treat others as equals. I feel like you're more like my friend than my teacher.

Hopefully, we can get together and have dinner sometime. That would be cool.

Mr. Millett: Had someone told me when I was six years old that we would be as close as we are now, I wouldn't have believed it. I first met you when I took dance lessons with your niece. She and I were such good friends, and she invited me to your house, where I first met you. I don't think I knew then that you used to swim with my mother or something. I didn't know you taught my brother either.

I remember one of the first days of middle school I was extremely anxious because I only knew about three people in my class. I felt much more relaxed when I heard your voice from 7B downstairs singing, "Wakey-wakey, eggs and bakey!" I recognized that voice, and in combination with the ridiculous words, I felt at home.

A week or two later, you were leading your class to lunch and I was walking down the hallway by myself. I reminded you who I was, and we had such a nice conversation that ended with my telling you that you should try out for American Idol, to which you replied, "Yeah, right. I think I could try out for 'American Scary-dol!'"

I didn't see you much for the next two years—partly because you went to Cony after I finished seventh grade. But I signed up for honors world history sophomore year and was in for the class of a lifetime.

First of all, the students in that class were amazing. We all gelled together and had a great time. But you were the rubber band that held us together. That class was so much fun. I could list all of the inside jokes, but this would be so much longer than it needs to be.

Every time you tell me you're going to miss me, it makes me sad because I'm going to miss you, like, six times more. Thank you so much for everything.

Mr. Wells: Yo mama! You are the teacher I most looked forward to having. Ever since I saw you in the school's production of Chizzle Wizzle when I was younger, in combination with my brother's stories about you, I yearned for the day that I would be sitting in your class.

Unfortunately, my enthusiasm and need to have you like me got in my way sophomore year. I tried way too hard to impress you. I was determined to make you like me, actually love me, but my method did not work, I guess. I worked so hard and tried to impress you, and ironically, this got in the way of sharing the real me. So sophomore year did not turn out like I wanted.

Things change junior year during AP lang.

Ever since I was in the second grade and we learned about voice, I've written the way I talk. My eighth-grade teacher, Mrs. Dawes, always said I wrote with sass. Unfortunately, most high school research papers are not supposed to be written with sass, but this changed my junior year in your class.

And this made all the difference.

Our focus was on rhetoric, and the myriad options writers have in order to capture their voice—their passion. This truly excited me, and junior year proved to be the most productive for me as a writer. Your own excitement about the written word ignited a fire in me that lay dormant for many years. Until I met you.

So, the beginning of junior year began on a positive note, but what made a huge difference was taking your creative writing class. In AP I was having a ball with rhetoric and capturing my voice, but something happened in creative writing that cemented our friendship. Since writing stories was a hobby of mine, I think I finally impressed you in the way I wanted. I will never forget the day I believe made all the difference.

Scene: Mr. Wells's room. Emily has just passed in her historical fiction paper about the assassination of John Lennon and is now waiting for a new assignment because she is ahead of everyone else.

Emily is sitting at her computer working on her next assignment. Mr. Wells sits at his desk and begins to read their assignments. About halfway through the class, Mr. Wells comes out of nowhere, stands in front of her desk, and then dramatically squats down until they are at eye level with one another. He stares at her with a serious look on his face. What seems like eternity passes, and he clears his throat and says, "I just read your paper. Thank you for saying 'album' instead of 'CD.'"

But honestly, you grew to be one of my favorite teachers of all time. We get along so well now. And I can proudly say that I have received two one-armed hugs from you. I'm not good at math, but I'm pretty sure that equals, like, one hug, which is more than I can say for a lot of people.

I just want you to know that my first book (or Oscar, because that's gonna happen) will be dedicated to you. I may not have been the best research paper writer; I may not have survived all the Wellsonian rubrics completely unscathed, but I do believe that you are proud of me.

And now I can die happily.

Last but certainly not least, **Mrs. Rodrigue**. Wow. This year with you has been, in one word—remarkable. I bonded with you faster than I did with Mrs. Tripp (and that only took a few days).

I remember the very first day of lit. I had done my summer assignment, but a tad differently than the rest of the class. I had lost the chart you passed out in June, so I made my own. I recall approaching you and asking if that was acceptable. You looked me dead in the face and said, "No, it's not. You will have to drop the class. The summer assignment is mandatory."

I felt like I was punched in the stomach. After all, this is my favorite subject.

You then said quickly, "Gotcha! I was only kidding. As a matter of fact, I admire you for taking the initiative to create your own chart. It looks better than mine."

And that was the start of our beautiful friendship.

I like to compare us to long-lost sisters finally meeting each other, slow-mo running into each other's arms. We sort of have twin telepathy—I mean look at our Apples to Apples games. We're two of a kind. Kindred spirits. Soul mates.

Do you remember when you offered (jokingly) to set me up with your son? OMG, how that made my day! Of course, the "only reason" you didn't do that was because he was oblivious or something, but it was cool anyway. You'd be the best mother-in-law ever.

Whether in class or at RAM time, you always taught us the best life lessons. I clearly recall you telling me, "Take a break from schoolwork and have fun while you still can," or, "There's nothing sexier than a man with a vacuum cleaner."

The best, and most heartwarming, day was when we were assigned a teacher about whom to write a bio for the school newspaper, the Rameses. One of my classmates raised her hand and asked, "Who is going to write your biography?"

You didn't hesitate. With a confident smile you replied, "Why, Emily, of course."

That makes me tear up each and every time I think about. (Sorry for the teardrop stain on this paper.) That was my proudest high school moment.

I still recall the last line of my article. "You will always be Teacher of the Year in my heart." Later I saw a video created by another student of yours who said the exact same thing. I was horrified that you might think I plagiarized that line, but I did not. It was just a strange coincidence, but when I think about it, you should be proud that so many students think this way about you.

I love you to the edge of the Milky Way and back ten times and back. As a matter of fact, I can honestly say, "I wanna be you when I grow up.

I love you and will miss you,
Emily

"Senior goodbyes: What a testimony to our faculty," I thought. Sitting in front of me was a paper that was six pages long, far beyond the "required" length. It was written by a senior in high school, who was about to graduate, a seventeen-year-old who had "senioritis." She felt it necessary to put her valuable time into thanking her teachers. She chose to dedicate enormous amounts of energy at the end of her senior year, when others were partying, finding ways to avoid work, and thinking of their boyfriends or girlfriends.

And Emily was not the only senior who did this. A large percentage of Laurie's seniors chose to go above and beyond the call of duty. Why?

Because teachers make a difference.

CHAPTER 18

Unexpected "Fringe Benefits"

With little doubt, the material pay for teachers is minimal, but the emotional satisfaction and meaningful difference makes it more than worth the countless hours we invest. On a more practical note, however, there are other benefits that aren't found in our contract. Students from years past continue to reward me in one way or another! On many occasions, I have profited from our meaningful relationships in ways that are quite amusing.

Thus far, many of my graduates have tried to "return the favor" when I run into them years later. They are excited at the opportunity to thank me for supporting them during their tumultuous years. For example, one who now is a salesperson at a local car dealership normally gives me large discounts when I buy an automobile from him. The script is always the same. I walk into the showroom and ask for him by name. He arrives and normally says, "Hey, Mr. Wells. How are you? I'm honored that you asked for me. What can I do for you?"

Normally, I shake his hand, pull him aside, and whisper in his ear, "Don't forget, you had better give me a good deal or I am going to announce to the entire staff what a challenge you were in class." This is always followed by a laugh, and then we are off to the car lot.

There, he helps me pick out the best deal. All the while we are talking excitedly and catching up. Then we return to the office and talk man to man, not man to *sales*man. Normally the conversation comes to the significant discount I'm receiving because of the relationship I created while he attended high school. (I visit other dealerships before coming to this one, so I know that I'm getting a deal.) It's always a wonderful experience, mainly because I have the opportunity to visit with a student of mine and also avoid the annoying bartering. Unlike most car customers, I enjoy the experience.

Another story comes to mind that humorously highlights the fringe benefits of teaching. I was driving my Prius to work early one morning (about 4:30), and while travelling through a small town, I approached a stop sign. I would normally slow down a bit, but I'd seldom stop, because it's so early and no one was around. The entire town was deserted, and I was in a hurry, so I just ran the stop sign. No sooner had I done this than a siren broke the early morning silence and blue lights pierced the darkness (remember, 4:30 a.m.).

"Crap," I said to myself. "That's all I need right now. I have a writing conference at 5:30 and I have work to do before that!"

Reluctantly, I grabbed my license and registration from the glove box and then rolled down my window. A pair of blue pants appeared at my open window; the officer never bent down to talk with me. From above came an authoritative voice.

"I take it you did not see that rather obvious stop sign back there. License and registration, please."

A large hand approached my open window and I forcefully placed my documents on the calloused skin. The voice announced, "Be right back, sir. Don't go anywhere."

I heard a car door slamming and waited in disgust for about five minutes before the police officer returned. This time, however, he leaned down, and a familiar face appeared. I really didn't recall the name that belonged to that face, but the words that came out of that mouth were wonderfully welcoming.

"Mr. Wells, you probably don't remember me, but I had you in class about fifteen years ago, when I was a junior at Cony. Back then I really did not have aspirations of becoming a police officer. In fact, I knew many of them personally, because, as you know, I was a wicked troublemaker. You, however, befriended me and served as a wonderful support system during bad times. You believed in me, and I worked harder for you than anyone. You are one of the major reasons why I am standing here today, with a good job and a good life. Thank you."

I replied, with a relieved smile on my face, "You are more than welcome. There must have been a good reason why I believed in you. I'm ecstatic that you have found your way."

He replied, "Without you, I would have ended up on the other side of the law. I was so fortunate to have you. So I am returning the favor. Today is your lucky day."

He returned my license and registration—nothing more. "Please stop next time," he said with a smile. "And God bless you," he added as he strolled away.

I sighed with relief at the prospect of keeping my driving record clean, but I experienced something that made me feel so damned good. I was filled with pride and fulfillment. I just wanted to scream:

I am a teacher and I make a difference!

My students end up in all walks of life, and I must admit that recently I was truly honored by one of them. Like the other episodes, it came as a surprise, and it also proved to me that there are fringe benefits to becoming a teacher. Yes, forming relationships and mentoring students is beyond satisfying, but I always embrace the opportunity to see them in the "real world" to celebrate their successes.

I was sitting in a small restaurant, which was also part of a pottery shop in Portland. I was about to have lunch with my twenty-three-year-old son Lucas, who sat across from me studying the menu. I heard footsteps approach, abruptly stopping at our table. The owner of the feet loudly cleared his throat. Thinking it was the waiter, I looked up from my menu and was happily surprised to see one of my favorite students from about four years ago.

"Dylan, how the heck are you?" I exclaimed.

He looked at me with a smirk on his face, replying, "Since when did you stop swearing? The old Mr. Wells would have said, 'How the *hell* are you?'"

My son Lucas laughed out loud at the comment, and then Dylan and I started gabbing away.

"What are you doing in a pottery shop? You don't have an artistic bone in your body, you old jock," Dylan delivered.

"Yeah, I know, but I am here to pick up some clay for my wife, and decided to take my son out to lunch at the same time." I looked at my boy and made the proper introduction: "Lucas, this is Dylan, one of my students of a few years back."

Lucas rolled his eyes. I knew he was growing tired of listening to my old students tell him how great a teacher I was. While he gave me his look, I continued the conversation.

"Why are you here? I don't remember you having anything to do with art either. You were a *hell* of a writer, but art? No way," I countered, feeling rather proud of myself. He wasn't going to get the best of me in front of Lucas.

I looked at Dylan and saw the same student I taught years ago. Excited at seeing him, and wanting to reconnect, I was about to ask a bunch of questions, but before I could, he announced, "I live in the upstairs apartment and graduated from the University of Southern Maine last May. Currently, I am working at Cushnoc Brewery while I apply to grad school. I really want to visit more, but I am on my way to work, and I can't be late. It was wonderful to see you."

Dylan shook my hand, then Lucas's, and sprinted out the door. I looked across the table at my boy, and he said, "Can't I go anywhere with you without running into someone who had you for a teacher?" He smiled, because he liked giving me a hard time, and then said, "No, really. I think it's cool that you had so many students who appreciated you. That must be very satisfying, despite the low pay."

We got back to our menus, when just a few short moments later, a rather large brown paper bag dropped from the sky. I looked up, and there was Dylan, with a mischievous grin on his face. Stepping back with authority, he announced, "This is a token of my appreciation for what you did for me in high school. I hope you enjoy it. Have a great day, Mr. Wells."

He walked out of the shop, while Lucas and I stared questioningly at the package that pretty much covered the small table. "What do you think is in there?" Lucas asked.

"Beats me. I'm not sure I should open it. Would you do it for me?" I responded.

"Sure, no prob." He reached out, unrolling the top of the bag and peering inside. Lucas lifted his head and stared at me with a huge grin on his face.

"What's so funny?" I asked him.

"I think I figured out one of the fringe benefits of teaching," he replied. "I think that Dylan truly appreciates you. Take a look at this," he said, opening the bag wide.

Gingerly, I reached out and separated the top sleeves. Slowly I peered into it, and what I saw made me laugh out loud. Inside, resting peacefully, was a half case of beer, representing various "flavors" produced by the brewery at which Dylan worked. I started laughing, feeling touched at the same time. I felt proud; I felt honored; I felt appreciated.

Just another of the many things that have happened that made me proud and thankful to have served so many students over the years.

There are far more "fringe benefits" to teaching, ones that make this profession a special one. People unfamiliar with teaching consider the summer vacations to be included on this list, which certainly is an attraction. It's wonderful to have this time to spend with family, doing things you love. There's little doubt that these breaks make teaching attractive, but these days off do not make up for the amount of time we spend in the classroom without students, planning our lessons, grading and scoring our assignments, meeting the new government requirements, or filling out myriad IEPs.

But the major benefit is the relationship we create with each and every student. I love watching them grow, watching their eyes light up when they finally understand something, and watching them when they receive their diploma and hold it up to the sky. I am now 64 years old, and I can honestly say I would not change a moment of my career. How many adults can say this?

CHAPTER 19

A Student Bares His Soul

Before I leave you with your thoughts, I must allow one of my students to "put a face" on the important points I have tried to make with the writing of this book. He best captures the integral role teachers play.

One of the many students for whom I made a difference was the 2018 salutatorian of Cony High School who wrote the following narrative. I chose him to share his story for a number of reasons. First and foremost, he is a brilliant writer, almost too good for this text. Secondly, despite the fact that he was a very successful student and also captain of the tennis team, he had serious issues that could have spelled disaster without the help of some of his teachers, along with a supportive family.

Prior to sharing his story, I must provide some background to this fine young man, Sean Tenney. I first met him his sophomore year—and I must admit—he made an impression. When he shyly entered my empty room, I think I stared at him for the longest time before saying, "Nice outfit. What's your name?"

He stood there, bright Hawaiian shirt contrasting with his plaid shorts, worn awkwardly on his slight, six-foot frame. Just below his knees stood a pair of colorful socks that travelled down his legs to set of red sneakers. Peering from below his large, round glasses framed by his brown Afro, he replied, "Good morning, Mr. Wells. My name is Sean Tenney."

He stuck out his hand and bowed, almost like he was worshipping me. He continued, "I have heard so much about you from my sister Ciara. She has spoken highly of you," he continued, almost in a whisper and bowing again.

He walked insecurely to an empty desk, sat down, and never said a word. Supporting his chin with his right hand, he stared intently at me with wide eyes buried beneath his geeky glasses. After the class filled with students and I began teaching, Sean would nod his head in agreement. He never spoke, however, unless solicited. When called on for an answer, he would always caress his chin with his right hand, stare pensively at the ceiling, and reply with a sentence that usually contained words I had never heard before. His classmates would either stifle their giggles or look at him like he was speaking a foreign language—and for some of them he was.

So, I guess you could call Sean socially awkward, especially since he was a sophomore taking a junior AP class. As the school year progressed, I learned that it was much more than that. It bordered on a phobia, paranoia, if you will. And of course, he did not feel comfortable around his classmates, who did not attempt to socialize with him, both because he was different and considerably more intelligent than they. After all, here was an awkward sophomore dressed for a Hawaiian wedding who was taking a junior AP class. His classmates did not necessarily taunt him, but they certainly did not attempt to make him feel at home early in the school year.

On the other hand, however, I *adored* him. Here was a very intelligent young man who dressed like an individual, not caring what others thought. I didn't realize at the time that he was struggling, battling demons of his own. He felt isolated, distant, the perfect definition of a social outcast. We became friends instantly, and I opened up my room to him unconditionally (as I would any student). During his lunch, he arrived, food in hand. We would have pleasant conversations while he ate, and after he went straight to work on his writing, which was his one and only love.

When stressed, he would visit my room, and unbeknownst to me, I was helping him through a tough time. I guess you could call me his mentor. After I retired, Laurie Rodrigue took over the role of Sean's "confidant." Together, we made an indelible impression on his life, and by the time Sean graduated salutatorian of his class, he represented a confident young man, secure in his persona, ready to go to college and make his mark on the world.

Watching him deliver his speech at the Civic Center in front of a couple of thousand people, I realized that he was a far cry from the freshman Sean Tenney, and he attributes much of his growth to not only his family, but also his supportive teachers who mentored him during his difficult times.

The insights he chose to share in this chapter capture the important influence teachers have on their students. In this case, he writes about me and Laurie Rodrigue, predominantly because he loved to write; it was his salvation, so to speak. Nonetheless, we helped to guide him from isolation. He wrote the following narrative, beginning in the third person, because that's the way he started as a freshman: an outsider.

What follows are the words of a struggling person. A kid who thought he had no one to talk to about the thoughts that warped his subconscious, that sapped joy. Written at random times during high school, they fill in the blanks, like annotations in the margins of a larger novel. They weren't intended as poetry. They were therapy. No one was ever supposed to read them.

But here they are. Exponents of assignments from his English classes, the only subject that seemed to settle his thoughts. Two teachers facilitated his work. They could have just applied red letters or soulless numbers across the top of a page. They could have discouraged his penchant to go on tangents, to just get to the point. To leave when class was dismissed.

But instead they encouraged him. They opened their classrooms for him during lunch hours. They became counselors, translating his teen soliloquies into focused, empathetic assessments.

They still don't know how deeply they connected with him. It's time I tell them.

Any person with experience in the secondary schooling system understands high school is about trying to survive. As a fifteen-year-old kid, I become determined to understand this period of life. I am treating adolescence as a subject to master, an academic discipline, a field of study. I believe that a whole domain of answers exists, embedded in teenagedom. My own journals could be a sort of Rosetta Stone. What for? I don't know. I couldn't tell you what my questions are, or what the answers I find would lead to. The pursuit is what matters; it is what consumes me.

My private search for personal truth illuminates my sleepless nights (the lights stay on, even when I turn them off), shadows my every action in the days I sleepwalk through. It overrides my capacity to socialize, to compete athletically, to perform in the classroom. The only joy I take in high school is from my English classes. These courses are the perfect release for a person who knows no other way.

My teachers were not obligated to be there for me to the extent they were. They translated my intense existential rants, always responding with nuanced, empathetic encouragement. They offered me things to think about, beyond the essays and literature they assigned. They sensed when I was struggling and accommodated me on the days I could barely function. They absorbed my problems and applied wisdom that helped me gain genuine clarity on them.

I can still recall early in sophomore year when Mr. Wells and I had a writing conference that cemented our relationship, one that would help me more than he would ever know. We sat in his room during lunch, and he was giving me his insights into my writing.

"Yes," he said, "you are very much behind the words. But you are not the words themselves. You don't seem to own them— not confidently, anyway. Your style is ripped from a dictionary. You don't communicate meaning clearly. You avoid articulating your opinion. Even when I tell you to write a story, I don't hear you in those paragraphs. You prefer abstract tangents to providing concrete evidence. Those modes of poetry are as close as I get to your personality, to your identity. You don't talk in class, so I don't know your voice yet. These conversations are my only exposure to you.

"What can I do to help you? Sean, the person. Forget Sean, the writer."

Those final words cleared the smoke. He had seen past my persona. I left quickly, but I returned with my lunch to his room, my eventual sanctuary—and it made all the difference.

After that, everything changed. I felt at home in room 2004, and my confidence grew. With Mr. Wells's mentorship, I grew into the person I am today, but it was gradual.

I kept my hair neater; my skin wasn't a sickly tone anymore; I didn't slouch. I had the confidence to calmly stop working on a paper, or test, when the time was up. During quizzes, I wouldn't piercingly glare at sources of interruption. I'd raise my hand more in class. I didn't opt to work alone on every group-optional in-class project. I grinned and waved at people in the hallways, eyeballing my feet less and less. I was allowing my classmates to become my friends. The teachers' feedback to my writing became synonymous with their reception to my overall human growth.

I had always had an identity in my writing. Now, I had identity in how I communicated, without a pencil or keyboard. An identity in how I moved, how I interacted with schoolmates and adults. I had always dressed colorfully. Now, other people were becoming aware of why this was: because behind those thick glasses and goofy socks was the spirit of a colorful person, who no longer spoke in a wary, grayscale whisper. My face wasn't a tight, emotionless mask. My fellow teenagers were seeing me for the first time—and I was one of them. My aura was flowering.

My classmates were realizing that I, too, was an adolescent; insecure and lovelorn and curious; giggly and innocent and playful. I finally could relate to them, and they to me. I told them stories of my awkwardness, sampling my personal life with a comic's delivery. These two teachers smiled at me with a knowing warmth, each day their professional detachment transforming to a mutual love. They told me they were proud of me. I was finally hearing voices other than those of my own creation, the ones that had threatened to end me.

That kid now sits in his bedroom, weeks after he's completed high school. He reviews his yearbook messages. He knows that those teachers deserve full credit for what is written in them—all the memories, adjectives, happy illustrations, x's and o's and emojis and phone numbers contained in those pages. Those experiences, feelings, and well-wishes would not have existed had they not intervened during times where his life was hardly alive. They regularly revived him. One of them called him a "survivor," deflecting his compliment that they were a "lifesaver." He wonders how he could adequately thank them for it all.

He then recalls what had bonded him with them in the first place. Without it, they would never have connected.

Writing.

Without it, they wouldn't have heard his voice. He remembers the prerequisites they taught him for any writing piece. He knows for what he is writing. He finally knows how, and definitely for whom. And, moreover, why. This, what you're reading, is his tribute letter to them.

But this letter is a confession. A confession of a teenager, struggling with himself, who eventually synchronized with an identity. The only proper conclusion is to claim this, own this, with my name.

This confession is from the Cony class of 2018's salutatorian. A varsity athlete and team captain. An active member of the school arts community and various extracurriculars. For all of the unresolved tension in my head, in my soul and subconscious, I was involved with my school. There weren't many outward signs that a great unhappiness had dominated me for all this time. But these two teachers, they knew. And they kept their discretion. Now, championing the autobiographical style as the hallmark of my art, I am ready to open up.

I am honored and humbled to be a contributor to this book. I am fulfilled that writing and sharing this has coincided with a developing inner peace. And I would not be here without those two educators. I wouldn't just be an absent entry from this book, or a suppressed anecdote.

I'd no longer be here at all.

Epilogue

So, what's my point? Am I trying to brag? Am I some crusty old fart who has nothing better to do than to focus on the past?

Not at all.

I am part of a fraternity of which I am most proud. Luckily, I am retired and have the time to reflect on my career. My students have taught me the most important lesson of my life: Good teachers play a vital role in their development, emotionally, academically, socially, and morally.

Although we are not fiscally rewarded for our role, our paycheck goes far beyond dollar signs. We must remember that our satisfaction comes from our clients, and this is far more important than anything else.

Teachers must continue this ever-important job and not lose sight of their mission. There has not been a time like this in the history of American education, and it's easy to get distracted and lose hope. When this happens, there is one and only one place educators should look… at their students sitting directly in front of them. Those kids know that good teachers play an integral role in their success and happiness.

They just proved it.

Thank You

I want to thank my students for playing an integral role in making my life meaningful and giving me the idea for this book. I'd also like to thank the Cony High School staff (and particularly Laurie Rodrigue) who donated their time to make this book a reality. The most important thank-you goes to my wife Martha for supporting me in my quest to become an effective teacher, loving husband, and supportive parent for our two sons, Max and Lucas.

About the Author

Photo by Steve Scoville

Born to a family of seven and raised in a small town in New York, Tom Wells graduated from Bates College in Lewiston, Maine in 1976. That day, he was informed that the Augusta School System wanted to hire him to teach English. He accepted their offer, and forty-one years later he captures his experience in his first book, Dear Mr. Wells. Along with the help of many of his students, he explores the teaching profession and its contribution to the development of a meaningful, confident individual. His own students, along with some "interesting" anecdotes, prove that an effective educator is a world-changer.